AFRICAN ETHNOGRAPHIC STUDIES OF THE 20TH CENTURY

Volume 6

THE MUGWE

THE MUGWE
A Failing Prophet

B. BERNARDI

LONDON AND NEW YORK

First published in 1959 by Oxford University Press for the International African Institute.

This edition first published in 2018
by Routledge
2 Park Square, Milton Park, Abingdon, Oxon OX14 4RN

and by Routledge
711 Third Avenue, New York, NY 10017

Routledge is an imprint of the Taylor & Francis Group, an informa business

© 1959 International African Institute

All rights reserved. No part of this book may be reprinted or reproduced or utilised in any form or by any electronic, mechanical, or other means, now known or hereafter invented, including photocopying and recording, or in any information storage or retrieval system, without permission in writing from the publishers.

Trademark notice: Product or corporate names may be trademarks or registered trademarks, and are used only for identification and explanation without intent to infringe.

British Library Cataloguing in Publication Data
A catalogue record for this book is available from the British Library

ISBN: 978-0-8153-8713-8 (Set)
ISBN: 978-0-429-48813-9 (Set) (ebk)
ISBN: 978-1-138-48918-9 (Volume 6) (hbk)
ISBN: 978-1-351-03834-8 (Volume 6) (ebk)

Publisher's Note
The publisher has gone to great lengths to ensure the quality of this reprint but points out that some imperfections in the original copies may be apparent.

Disclaimer
The publisher has made every effort to trace copyright holders and would welcome correspondence from those they have been unable to trace.

M. Mugambi (left), the Mugwe of the Igembe, and Muruku, the retired Mugwe. See page 32.

THE MUGWE,
A FAILING PROPHET

A STUDY OF A RELIGIOUS AND PUBLIC
DIGNITARY OF THE MERU OF KENYA

BY

B. BERNARDI, I.M.C.

With a Foreword by DARYLL FORDE

Published for the
INTERNATIONAL AFRICAN INSTITUTE
by the
OXFORD UNIVERSITY PRESS
LONDON NEW YORK TORONTO
1959

Oxford University Press, Amen House, London E.C.4
GLASGOW NEW YORK TORONTO MELBOURNE WELLINGTON
BOMBAY CALCUTTA MADRAS KARACHI KUALA LUMPUR
CAPE TOWN IBADAN NAIROBI ACCRA

© International African Institute, 1959

PRINTED IN GREAT BRITAIN BY THE WHITEFRIARS PRESS LTD.
LONDON AND TONBRIDGE

FOREWORD

Father Bernardi has, as he explains in his Introduction, undertaken a study of a ritual office which has been of great social significance among the Meru of the Central Province of Kenya. The role of the Mugwe among the Meru tribes had received little attention in the earlier literature and its character had been little appreciated, if not misunderstood. The Meru, seeking analogies in other societies, have likened the Mugwe to a king or to a bishop. As Father Bernardi shows, the character of this office cannot be adequately presented in such terms, for analysis of the type and range of authority embodied in the Mugwe requires close study of the indigenous social system of the Meru and of the moral and cultural values it sustained. On this basis he is able to make significant comparisons with ritual dignitaries of some other East African peoples, notably the Laibon among the Masai, and the Hayu or Abba Boku of the Boran Galla. That the functions of the Mugwe were so deeply rooted in the values of the traditional way of life also serves to explain their inevitable decline with the growth of new interests and the transformation of the social framework under changed political and economic conditions.

Father Bernardi has had a long experience among African peoples and he has pursued advanced studies in the University of Rome and the University of Cape Town, at both of which he was awarded a Doctorate. His earlier publications include 'The Social Structure of the Kraal among the Zezuru in Musami, Southern Rhodesia' (1950), 'The Age-System of the Nilo-Hamitic Peoples' (*Africa*, October 1952), and *Le Religioni dei Primitivi*

FOREWORD

(1953). Since 1953 he had been attached to the Catholic Mission at Nkubu in the Diocese of Meru. This afforded him the opportunity of visiting all the Meru sub-tribes, establishing close relations with many holders of the office of Mugwe. The International African Institute was happy to be able to make him a grant for field research that gave him the opportunity of pursuing more intensive studies among the Meru. This he did over a period of nine months in 1955 and a shorter period in 1956. The present volume is a product of that work and will, it is hoped, significantly advance the understanding of East African peoples and the study of their religious institutions.

The Institute is itself indebted to the Ford Foundation for a grant which has enabled it to provide for its current programme of field research and to publish studies resulting from it. Its thanks are also due to the Bishop of Meru and to Father Bernardi's religious superiors of the Consolata Catholic Mission for releasing him from other duties while carrying out these researches.

DARYLL FORDE
Director,
International African Institute

London, October 1958

INTRODUCTION

The present work is based on material recorded mostly during a tour of nine months field work among the Meru of Kenya, as a Research Fellow of the International African Institute, from April to December, 1955. Before that, thanks to the generous assistance of my religious superiors, I had been able to study the Meru at various times since 1953, while I was attached to the staff of the Catholic Mission, Nkubu, in the Diocese of Meru.

At first the scope of my work was limited to the study of the social structure of the Tharaka with special reference to their Mugwe. But I soon realized that in order to assess the significance and position of the Mugwe, my enquiry must be extended to the other Meru sub-tribes, who also acknowledge the authority of the Mugwe. In the past, the importance of the Mugwe among the Meru sub-tribes was certainly very great. It has now been declining owing to the many changes that have been brought about during the last decades. My research came slightly late to be able to record all the aspects of the Mugwe as an institution, though not too late, as I was fortunate enough to record oral traditions and statements by the elders, and also to contact personally the living Mugwe of most Meru sub-tribes.

I have always been struck by the vigour with which my informants maintained that the Mugwe was their leader and that they could recognize no other but the Mugwe. Chiefs are of a different order: they are there because of the Government, but the Mugwe is the Mugwe.

The Mugwe was frequently likened to the King: ' He is our King, he is like the Kabaka of Uganda.' This, indeed,

viii INTRODUCTION

was the first description of the Mugwe that I heard. Later the simile became a familiar one as I recorded it again and again, especially among the Tharaka and the Chuka, and I discovered that the same description had been noted by other investigators, long before me.

Mr. H. E. Lambert told me how his informant, the late chief the Rev. Philip M. Inoti[1] of the Methodist Mission, described the Mugwe in these words: 'The Mugwe is like the King, or better, he is like the Archbishop.'

The Rev. Fr. E. Cavicchi, I.M.C., recalls how at Imenti Mission, during 1946, he was once present at a history class and he heard the teacher, Isidoro M. Muthamia, compare the Mugwe 'to the King of the English and the Kabaka of the Baganda '.

So many similar statements, made in such different circumstances of time, place and persons, leave no doubt as to the importance of the institution they seek to describe. In fact, the Mugwe is neither a king nor a bishop, but there is no doubt that the institution he represents is one of the basic and most firmly established elements of the old structure of Meru social life. The nature of his office is at the same time religious and secular. In Meru society, as in all human societies, it is not possible to draw a clearcut distinction between the religious and the secular. The two conceptions intermingle and are so intimately associated in real life, especially in primitive societies, that they both constitute the theoretical basis of action and the constitutional foundation of the social structure. Bearing this in mind, the value of statements describing the Mugwe as 'the centre of all Meru social

[1] The initial M. stands for *Muntu*, man. It is a general custom of the Meru to give a man this title after his initiation to manhood, which is regarded as an honour. Though the initial M. is used in writing, pronunciation is *Nto*, which is a contracted sound from the original *muntu*. The correct shortened form should be N., not M., which, however, is now the accepted one.

INTRODUCTION ix

life' will be understood. He is also called *kajene* or 'the queen of the bees': around him all the Meru assemble; for him they work; him they protect. In return, the presence of the Mugwe is a guarantee for the continuity of the people and for the prosperity of the country. He is also described as 'the foundation stone of the Meru structure', *ni we gitina kia Meru*.

There are also other names by which the Meru refer to the Mugwe: *munene, mutungeria, mutuguni*, chief, leader, benefactor. He is also called 'the custodian of the Country', 'the messenger of God', and even 'our God', because his actions are as good as if they were the actions of God. It seems, therefore, that the best rendering in English of the term Mugwe is the word prophet, in the sense of a man who, inspired by God, leads his people.

Mugwe, pl. *Agwe*, is a name of honour. Its spelling in the singular is the same as in the word *mugwe*, pl. *migwe*, which means 'arrow' in a general sense. However, the stress and the tone of the two words are different. *Mugwe/Agwe* has no special stress, and its stem *-gwe* has an open tone. Its pronunciation is, therefore, *mogwe*. (Among the Igembe and the Tigania the *g-* sound is dropped, consistently with their variance from other Meru dialects, and the word is pronounced *mowe*.) In *mugwe/migwe*, the stem *gwe* is stressed and has a closed tone. The pronunciation is *mogwé/megwé*.

The word *Mugwe/Agwe*, at present, has no literal significance. Besides being an official designation, it can be used with reference to a very good person, well born and courteous. This use, however, is rare.

Ugwe is the abstract term indicating the power of the Mugwe.

Since the coming of the Europeans to Meru, many changes have taken place. More have occurred during the Mau

Mau Emergency, and the tide is still mounting. The institution of the Mugwe has suffered most. What was, without doubt, part and parcel of the old system has not stood up to the impact of the new way of life that has overwhelmed the Meru. There are many causes of the present decline of the Mugwe. Being like the queen of the bees, he was concealed from the newcomers in order to ensure his survival. He has, in consequence, been ignored. The existence of the Mugwe has become an item of esoteric knowledge.

Up to now no published literature has been available on the Mugwe. Mr. H. E. Lambert, a distinguished scholar and a former District Commissioner of the Meru, has written a section on the Mugwe in a major work on the Meru that is still awaiting publication. I read this section at Mr. Lambert's house in Nairobi, and it gives me pleasure to acknowledge my debt to him and to thank him also for his experienced advice in the early stages of my fieldwork.

I wish also to thank Bishop L. V. Bessone, I.M.C., the first Bishop of Meru, and all the Consolata Fathers for their fraternal assistance and hospitality. The confidence that the Fathers enjoy with their people was a very great help to my work, especially in breaking down the atmosphere of suspicion due to the Mau Mau Emergency.

I owe a special debt of gratitude to the Rev. Father E. Cavicchi, I.M.C. He gave freely of his intimate knowledge of the Meru, and there are few points that he did not discuss with stimulating criticism.

My thanks are also due to the Executive Council of the International African Institute for the honour of granting me one of their Fellowships, and personally to Professor V. L. Grottanelli, who first suggested that I should apply for it.

INTRODUCTION xi

Finally, I should mention my devoted assistant and old pupil, Cornelio M. Mbijiwe, for his intelligent contributions; and the many elders from all Meru sub-tribes, especially the Agwe, who volunteered their information with so much patience and understanding.

To the memory of Sister Eugenia, murdered by Mau Mau terrorists at Imenti Mission on the 28th September, 1953, and to the Rev. Father Cavicchi, who suffered seriously in the same attack, this book is humbly dedicated.

B. B.

CONTENTS

FOREWORD   v

INTRODUCTION   vii

Chapter One. THE MERU

1. The sub-tribes 1
2. The Meru dual divisions 9
3. The clan system 11
4. The age-set system 17
5. The *njuri* association 24
6. Changing agencies 28

Chapter Two. VISITING THE AGWE

1. The prophet and the diviner in Igembe . . . 31
2. The Mugwe and the Mukiama of the Tigania . . 35
3. The situation and the residence of the Imenti Mugwe 38
4. The Mugwe of the Tharaka 40
5. The Mugwe and the Assistant Agwe of the Chuka . 43
6. The diviner of the Muthambi, Mwimbi, etc. . . 46
7. Among the Mbere 47
8. Some indicative patterns 48

Chapter Three. MYTHOLOGICAL ORIGINS OF THE UGWE

1. In the beginning 52
2. The exodus 56
3. Some cultural heroes of the Meru 62
4. The first Mugwe 67
5. The identification of the Agwe with the first Mugwe 69
6. Some beliefs and sayings about the Mugwe . . . 72
7. The Ugwe and the Meru 75

Chapter Four. 'BORN TO BE MUGWE' (*Mugwe we ni guciarwa*)

1. The original family unity of the Agwe 77
2. The hereditary principle and the right of primogeniture 82
3. The training of a candidate for the office of Mugwe . 86

xiv CONTENTS

4. The death of the Mugwe and the accession of his
  successor 88
5. The insignia of the Mugwe 94

Chapter Five. THE POWER OF THE MUGWE

1. The moral virtues of the Mugwe 105
2. The blessing of the Mugwe 110
3. The sanctions and curses of the Mugwe . . . 118
4. The Mugwe as judge 122
5. 'The Ugwe is from God' 123
6. The Mugwe and the *mugaa* 128
7. The Mugwe and his divining activity 131
8. Prophet rather than priest 136

Chapter Six. THE POSITION OF THE MUGWE
IN THE SOCIAL STRUCTURE

1. In the sub-tribe 141
2. In the clan, lineage, and family 147
3. The Mugwe and the elders 150
4. The Mugwe and the warriors 155
5. The theoretical significance and position of the Mugwe
  in the social structure 157
6. Some comparative figures:
   (*a*) The Laibon of the Masai 162
   (*b*) The Hayu or Abba Boku of the Galla Boran 165

Chapter Seven. THE FAILING PROPHET

1. Concealing the Mugwe 169
2. Changing attitudes 174
3. M. Kiganka of the Chuka 177
4. The vacancy in Imenti 181
5. The Mugwe of the Tharaka 182
6. The Mugwe of the Igembe and of the Tigania . . 184
7. Different reactions to the present changes . . . 186

APPENDIX: Some Select Documents and Narrations 191

BIBLIOGRAPHY 205

INDEX 207

PLATES

M. Mugambi, the Mugwe of the Igembe,
and Muruku, the retired Mugwe   *Frontispiece*

1a.   M. Ruanda, the Mugwe of the Tharaka   *facing page* 80

1b.   A group of Imenti youngsters   ,,   ,,   80

2a.   M. Kiganka, the Mugwe of the Chuka   ,,   ,,   81

2b.   M. Muga, the blind elder, and Nkeya, the
old circumciser of the Tharaka   ,,   ,,   81

3.   M. Lunyiru, the diviner of the Igembe   ,,   ,,   112

4.   M. Kamunde, with all his professional tools ,,   ,,   113

Map : Tribes of Meru District and sur-
rounding country   ,,   ,,   1

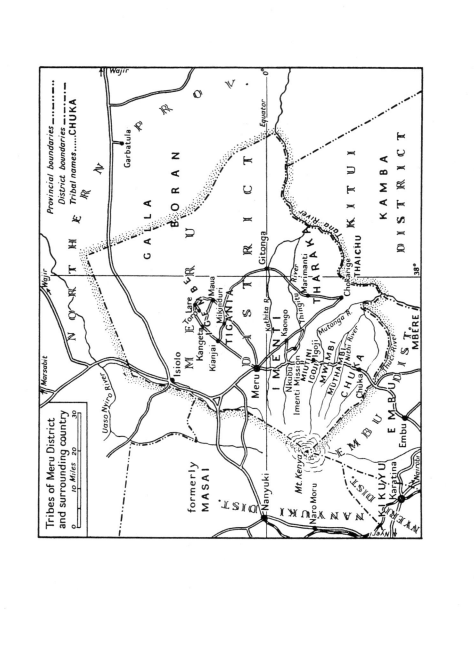

Chapter One

THE MERU

1. THE SUB-TRIBES

The Meru are a Bantu tribe and live mainly in the District of Meru of the Central Province of Kenya. Since the beginning of 1956, they have been separated from the Kikuyu to form the Meru Land Unit. The proclamation of this special Land Unit constitutes an official acknowledgement of the present tribal unity of the Meru, distinct territorially, linguistically and socially, from the Kikuyu and the Embu. The Meru number about 300,000.

The geographical distribution of the Meru coincides almost entirely with the administrative boundaries of the District of Meru. The Thagichu or Thaichu, a section of the Tharaka, is the only group outside the District. They live on the eastern side of Tana River and form a Location of Kitui District, Ukamba.

The District Commissioner of Meru resides at Meru Town, a progressive trading centre. The District is divided into 4 Divisions and 16 Locations and a number of Sub-Locations, as follows:

1. *Nithi Division:* Mwimbi Location, Muthambi Loc., Kiringani Loc., Magumoni Loc.
2. *North Imenti Division:* Upper Abothoguci Loc., Miiriga Mieru Loc., Lower Abothoguci Loc.
3. *South Imenti Division:* Nkuene Loc., Igoji Loc., Tharaka Loc.
4. *Nyambeni Division:* Kianjai Loc., Mikinduri Loc., Muthara Loc., Maua Loc., Kangeta Loc., Akaciu Loc.

THE MUGWE, A FAILING PROPHET

Each division is supervised by a Divisional District Officer; each location is controlled by a District Officer assisted by a Chief; there is one Headman for each sub-location.

The District Commissioner is advised by the African District Council, a board of nominated councillors of which the Commissioner is the president *ex officio*. A recent reform has added to the council a number of delegates from the *njuri* from every Location. The *njuri* are members of an indigenous council of elders with legal powers (see below, p. 24). The inclusion of the *njuri* in the District Council should provide an easier way for the administrator to test the temper of the people and an effective means to explain to them all the various reforms and by-laws passed by the council.

All the Meru state that they came to their present country after migration. They share this tradition with the other bordering Bantu peoples, the Kikuyu, the Embu, the Mbere and the Kamba. It is very probable that these people once formed a single group, occupying the same territory, whence they moved, splitting up at different stages on the way. For our present purpose it is of no consequence to trace all these movements in more detail. We refer the reader to Lambert's work.[1]

Generally the Meru, with the exception of the Chuka who regard the forests of Mount Kenya as their original abode, are consistent in saying that the place from which they moved was called Mbwa, though other names are also mentioned. Mbwa seems to refer to a land beyond an expanse of water that the emigrants had to cross. In my evidence, the north, and not the east, is the direction from which the migration came out. The term used is *urio*, literally meaning the right-hand, but geographically

[1] Lambert, 1950. (See Bibliography.)

THE MERU   3

interpreted for north. The point is open to conjecture as
one hears many contradictory statements from all the
Meru sub-tribes. The facts that can be taken as established in the tradition are that the Meru arrived in their
present country from a place where they were held in a
state of subjugation, if not of actual slavery; and that their
exodus was organized by a great leader. There are many
versions of the event. It is of interest to note that a number
of these versions name the first Mugwe as that leader
(see Chapter III).

Though now, more than ever, the Meru form a single
tribe, a number of tribal sections or sub-tribes must still
be distinguished on account of their many peculiarities,
dialectal differences, variations in the initiation ceremonies and other social institutions, territorial and residential distances, and past histories. The district divisions and
other administrative units do not coincide with these
sub-tribes.

There are nine Meru sub-tribes: the *Igembe, Tigania,
Imenti, Miutini, Igoji, Mwimbi, Muthambi, Chuka, Tharaka.*
A detailed account of their traditional history has been
published by Mr. H. E. Lambert to whose work we have
already referred the reader. The brief description that
follows will be limited to a few indications that are thought
pertinent to a study of the institution of the Mugwe. My
remarks are based on evidence I have collected personally.
They generally agree with Lambert's material.

The *Igembe* live on the Nyambene range in the north
of the District where they have remained more or less
isolated. For this reason they have clung doggedly to
their traditional way of life which has been preserved
more genuinely than by any other of the Meru sub-
tribes. During recent years there has been great
interest in education, and an increased volume of trade,

4   THE MUGWE, A FAILING PROPHET

both trends of some promise. The Igembe have some trade contact with the bordering Galla-Boran of the northern plains. At Mutuate and Maua markets it is common to see the Boran exchanging their sheep for Igembe cereals. The Igembe are part of the Nyambene Division with three locations: Maua, Kangeta, Akaciu. In the census of 1948 they numbered 49,604.

The *Tigania* extend over the plains which lie between the Imenti forest and the southern slopes of the Nyambene. Their land offers good grazing, and the Tigania are richer in cattle than all other Meru. In 1948 they numbered 48,496. The Tigania are also part of the Nyambene Division with three Locations: Kianjai, Mikinduri, Mutharia.

The *Imenti* are spread over the area, crossed by the Equator, between the north-eastern slopes of Mt. Kenya and the upper Imenti forest. They constitute the most compact group and the main bulk of the Meru. As a whole they are to be considered as the most progressive of the Meru sub-tribes, though some marginal sections have tended to remain backward. Meru Town lies in the Imenti area. Goodwill and co-operation between the Administration and the Missions have been effective in implementing reforms and in improving substantially their old way of life. In 1948 the Imenti numbered 91,366. They are administered within the two Imenti Divisions, except for the Igoji and Tharaka Locations in the South Imenti Division.

The *Muthambi, Mwimbi, Igoji,* and *Miutini* reside in the area between the Imenti and the Chuka. These small groups have no very definite tradition of their own and are said to be related, the Miutini to the Chuka, the others to the Imenti. But the other Meru often regard them as a whole group, quite distinct from themselves:

THE MERU

Miutini, Igoji, Mwimbi, Muthambi ni antu bamwe: ' they are one '. With regard to the Mwimbi, who form the most numerous of these small sub-tribes, there is a strong tradition in Imenti which says that they were not Meru, though they managed to infiltrate among the Meru and settled on their present lands. This view is supported by the information that the Imenti regarded the Mwimbi as their enemies in the same way as the Masai and the Mbere. Coffee, which does very well on their fertile land, has become a regular and substantial cash-crop for all these sub-tribes who are considered economically the most prosperous of all the Meru. The Mwimbi and the Muthambi each form a Location of the Nithi Division; the Igoji, together with Miutini, form the Igoji Location of the South Imenti Division. In 1948 the whole group numbered 33,800, the Mwimbi alone being 19,000.

The *Chuka* live on the south-eastern slopes of Mt. Kenya, and cover the area between the Thuci River in the south, and the Nithi River in the north. It is a common tradition with the Chuka that they have always been in the forests of Mt. Kenya whence they moved down to their present abode. Other versions of the Chuka migratory tradition say that they came out from Mbwa with the other Meru. I found also that the Chuka are believed to have sprung from the Tharaka. They have also a form of blood-brotherhood with the Igembe and the Tigania. On the other hand there are some customs, as, for instance, the method of circumcision, by which the Chuka may be assimilated to the Embu. One may be correct in considering the Chuka as primarily Meru who, having climbed the first slopes of Mt. Kenya, clearing the forest for cultivation (even at present the fields of the Chuka are on the lower section of their country), mixed with the aboriginal inhabitants of the forest and established some kind

6 THE MUGWE, A FAILING PROPHET

of contact with the Embu. These aboriginal forest inhabitants seem to have been the Gumba, now only remembered by some traditions and described as very small people. It seems certain that they were a pygmy race.

Of the Meru District, the Chuka are those who have suffered most the impact and violence of Mau Mau rebellion. During the Emergency they were the only Meru to be forcibly settled into villages of the Kikuyu and Embu pattern. Recently, however, they have been allowed to return to their fields, as before. The Chuka are part of the Nithi Division with two Locations, Kiringani and Magumoni. In 1948 they numbered 18,480.

The *Tharaka* are spread over the rocky hills from the plains around the Nyambene Range down to the Tana, Mutonga, and Githimu Rivers. The Thagichu, as mentioned, live beyond the Tana in Kitui District. Social intercourse between the main section of the Tharaka and the Thagichu has never been broken off, thanks to a continuous exchange of trade at local markets. Trade between the Kamba and the Tharaka is also steady.

The position of the Tharaka in relation to the other Meru has always been a matter of speculation and discussion. In fact I have found that they hold the same traditions as the Imenti and other sub-tribes with whom they claim to have come from Mbwa. E. R. Shackleton[1] mentions the Nguve as the early inhabitants of the present land of the Tharaka, by whom they were finally assimilated. The Nguve are described as pastoralists who did not practise circumcision. They are not, generally, remembered by the present-day Tharaka.

I have found no special evidence to support the theory that the Tharaka are the product of off-shoots of various clans and tribes; on the contrary, I have been surprised

[1] See Bibliography.

by the consciousness of tribal unity possessed by the Tharaka even in relation to the other Meru. They say: *Meru ni bamwe*, 'all Meru are one'; and also: *Tharaka ni bamwe*, ' all Tharaka are one'. The Tharaka have a system of clans, tribal ceremonies, age-units and also age-classes, based on the same general pattern as other Meru. Much of the residential instability of the Tharaka, noted in several Political Reports of Meru District, is due to the low average rainfall and the need for the Tharaka, who are still bound to the digging stick, to move in search of a fresh piece of land which can yield a richer crop of millet. Millet is their staple food. They also keep bee-hives and generally do very well with honey which is collected twice in the year. During the Mau Mau Emergency a District Officer has been posted among the Tharaka, and a Missionary priest has taken up residence at Materi Catholic Mission, not far from the central market at Chokarige. Their presence will certainly help the progress of the Tharaka. The Tharaka Location is part of the South Imenti Division. In my experience I have found the Tharaka intelligent, generally grateful, and some-times even generous, though their social life appears to be too frequently embittered by personal ill-feelings or *fitina*. The 1948 census gave their numbers as 16,505.

In spite of the above divisions it is not incorrect to consider all the Meru sub-tribes as a single tribe. The first reason is the assertion of the fact by the Meru themselves. There seems to be no doubt, however, that the tribal unity of the Meru in the past was of a territorial, social and linguistic rather than of a political nature. There were such social institutions as the age-class system and, within it, the *njuri* association and councils which provided a basis for fuller social intercourse with possible political consequences above the level of the sub-tribe.

8   THE MUGWE, A FAILING PROPHET

Besides these, there was no political authority having power over the tribe as a whole. There was one Mugwe for each sub-tribe, except for the Mwimbi and the other small sub-tribes that cluster round them. Each Mugwe possessed the same power, the Ugwe, for his own territory. The plurality of the Agwe and their territorial distribution does not prevent the elders from saying that *ugwe ni bumwe*, ' the power of the Ugwe is one '.

The present situation is different. The administration has strengthened the unity of the Meru and the setting up of a centralized machinery for the district government has been the means of fostering tribal unity. The enhanced authority of the *njuri* who have now been called, as already mentioned, to be members of the District Council, has contributed much to its effectiveness. The aim of the Government has been primarily administrative, but since the Emergency it has taken steps to separate the Meru from any association with the Kikuyu. The Meru now possess a consciousness of their tribal unity to the opposition and exclusion of other similar or neighbouring units; a consciousness far greater than in the past when the opposition was directed towards the inner sections or sub-tribes.

Indeed, the working units of all activities, religious, social, and political, were, and, for the most part, still are, the sub-tribes. It is within their structure that the indigenous institutions must first be analysed. At the same time one must not lose sight of the basic unity of all the Meru, for if investigation did not extend over and above the sub-tribal level, one would fail to understand the true nature and value of Meru structural institutions.

THE MERU

2. THE MERU DUAL DIVISIONS

Groups in the Imenti sub-tribe have names that refer to the tribe's crossing of the water on their way from Mbwa. According to the intensity of the light while they were crossing, people were called *njiru*, 'black', *ntune*, 'red', and *njeru*, ' white '. (See the full account in Chapter III.) All the clans were named after their own colour: *miiriga miiru*, the black clans; *miiriga mitune*, the red clans; *miiriga mieru*, the white clans. It seems certain that in the past the distinction may have had some effective territorial, social, and, very probably, political significance. Certainly, at present, it is of no social importance among the Imenti. The name *Miiriga Mieru* is preserved as a name of the Location around Meru Town, in North Imenti Division. The elders of the Imenti still say that there was really no distinction between the *miiriga miiru* and the *miiriga mitune;* they formed a single group. This suggests a possible adjustment of the original names to a dual division which has now entirely lost its significance, but which seems to have been typical in one form or other for all the Meru sub-tribes.

(*a*) Taking the Imenti first, they are said to have been divided into two groups, the *Nkuene* and the *Igoki*. The groups were territorial, the Nkuene being on the south, the Igoki on the north. Nowadays, the two terms survive as names of clans; Nkuene is also the name of the only Location, in the South Imenti Division, actually including a section of the Imenti sub-tribe. The Igoki group seems to have included all ' the white clans, *miiriga mieru* ', and the two terms appear to have become synonymous.[1] The

---

[1] An Imenti elder gave the following description of the Igoki to Father Cavicchi : 'The Igoki were very proud ; they wanted always to be the first in grazing and watering their cattle. The *Miiriga Mitune* resented this. Finally the latter declared war, defeated them, and forced them up into the area of Mutindwa (Meru Town).'

10 THE MUGWE, A FAILING PROPHET

two divisions were also referred to geographically: those of *urio*, north, those of *umotho*, south.

(*b*) A similar dual division, *Urio* and *Umotho*, is also found among the Tharaka. It was only mentioned, however, with relation to the Mugwe.

The Mugwe, I was told, is from those of *Umotho*. Those of *Urio* were the children of a Mugwe's 'sister', but they also must comply with all the orders issued by the Mugwe. I collected a list of seventeen clans of *Umotho*, and of fourteen clans of *Urio*. When I checked their territorial relation, I found that people who described themselves as of *Umotho* had their house close to people of *Urio*. It was possible, however, to note a prevalence of the groups in some areas: those of *Umotho* are mostly found in the area of Kamanyaki, Kamothanga and Kijige; those of *Urio* in the areas of Mpunja, Karukuni, and Thagichu. I was told also that in the past, after a successful raid, the booty was divided among the warriors according to their membership of the *Umotho* and *Urio* divisions. With regard to marriage there are no exogamic regulations with reference to these divisions: 'All the Tharaka are one.'

(*c*) Among the Igembe I did not find any special dual division except the alternating divisions (p. 21) of the age-classes. The only mention of *Urio* and *Umotho* refers to the distribution of huts in a polygynous homestead: the first wife is always of *Urio*, the right.

(*d*) The Tigania distinguish between the *Athwana* and the *Igoki*. The Athwana seems to be larger than the Igoki. I counted more than twenty-eight clans as Athwana in Kianjai Location and partly in Muthara, while the Igoki are most found in Mikinduri Location and partly in Muthara Location. The two divisions are also referred to

THE MERU

as *Umotho* for Athwana, and *Urio* for Igoki. As we shall see further on, the Mugwe of the Tigania resides among the Igoki. The Athwana, on the other hand, have another dignitary called Mukiama.

(*e*) The Chuka are also said to have been divided into two groups, the *Thagana* and the *Tumbiri*. I made special enquiries on this point but I was unable to find any trace of this division; in my evidence Thagana is the name of an unimportant clan; Tumbiri is still mentioned as a name of a place. The Chuka do not attach any special significance to the terms *Urio* and *Umotho*.

Thus we find that the dual division, at least among the Tharaka and the Tigania, bears some relation to the presence of the Mugwe (and the Mukiama), which seems to indicate that the dual division might in the past have had some social and political significance.

3. THE CLAN SYSTEM

Even at present, the clan, *mwiriga* pl. *miiriga*, is the most important unit in all Meru social functions and relations.

It is difficult, now, to distinguish a clan territorially. C. Dundas,[1] in 1915, described the Tharaka as follows: 'they are clearly divided into clans residing each in its own area', but he also saw evidence that 'the breaking-up of the clans has perhaps already commenced.' Throughout Meruland it is sometimes possible to note how members of one clan outnumber all other inhabitants of the same area. Unoccupied land is still described in terms of clan ownership, for land is, in fact, owned corporately by clans. This statement must be explained. The ownership of the land by clans does not prevent the individual from being the 'owner', but is in the nature of a sovereign ownership to which all land reverts directly if it remains

[1] See Bibliography.

12 THE MUGWE, A FAILING PROPHET

without any individual owner; in the same way land cannot be alienated from the clan except by an act of the clan. The consent of the individual owner must always be obtained if land is to be taken from him or if he is asked to surrender some for a common purpose. Full consideration is given to individual rights: *kigai gia kaiji gitingitunyua*, ' the hereditary estate of a small boy can never be absorbed ', is a principle of common law.

Clans are exogamous units. Exogamy, however, may be enforced only between the sub-clans or the lineages that are all units called by the same term *mwiriga*. On the other hand, marriage between all clan-units may be barred by special prohibitions such as blood-brotherhood (*giciaro*), parental curses (*irumi*), or traditional feuds.

Clan membership is basically obtained by birth, but it becomes a personal right by social acquisition. Among the Tharaka, for instance, I was told that a boy is not considered a member of the clan until he is married: in fact, it is only at that time that he leaves his father's homestead and goes to live on his own. Marriage gives him personal property, i.e. land for cultivation and cattle.

Clans are also ceremonial and political units. Ceremonial and political activities bring out the corporate unity of the clan, especially in such cases as fines for murder or adultery, when all members of the clan are expected to contribute to the payment simply because of their membership of that clan. They may also be defendants in a case brought against any one of them.

(*a*) *The elders.* The clan is actually represented by its elders. It is they who control all the corporate activity of the clan, ceremonial and political, both within the clan and with reference to other clans. Initiation is always a

THE MERU   13

ritual performed within a family or a group of families, but it cannot be held unless the candidate's father has secured the elder's permission. The elders have a right to a portion of the bridewealth, both in meat and beer, when marriage is legally solemnized. The purificatory sacrifice of a goat that follows a death must be attended and performed by the clan elders. It is also the elders who have to decide if and when a sacrifice is required to call down rain on the fields. This ceremonial power of the clan elders is not to be confused with the sacrificial power of the very old men, *ntindiri*, whose privilege it is to perform religious ceremonies for the whole tribe or sub-tribe.

The position of the elders within the clan is equally stressed by the political activity of the clan. Disputes are heard by a council of elders, who have power to pass judgement and enforce it by fines and even by corporal punishment. Sentence of death could not apparently be passed by the elders of a single clan, but was a matter for a general council of all the elders of a place (*rutere*), and more specifically of the *njuri*.[1]

(*b*) *The agambi.* The elders of the clan possess, basically, equal rights. Their authority is defined by their status which, in its turn, is defined by a number of other elements, age-class membership or seniority, wealth and wisdom. The *agambi* (speakers), the most important of all, are the actual leaders of the clan in all matters. The status of a *mugambi*, ' the possessor of the word ', is recognized as a distinction. His ability to lead a discussion makes it possible for him to sway the opinion of his fellow-elders and bend them to his own will. A *mugambi* is trained

---

[1] A capital sentence could be carried out in several ways: by burning the guilty man under a huge cover of dry banana leaves; or by drowning in a waterfall into which the culprit was thrown with his hands tied at the back to a stone; or by tying him on to an ant's nest to be eaten by the insects.

14 THE MUGWE, A FAILING PROPHET

informally, though individually, from boyhood. The choice is made entirely on personal gifts. A boy may have been observed to possess natural qualities of intelligence, shrewdness and strength. He is, therefore, singled out from among the others and is asked, either by his father or his sponsor, to attend the meetings of the elders, while still a boy. He should keep silent, but will learn by listening and observing. As a young initiate, *muthaka*, he will be selected as a member of the inner councils of the initiates, *nthaka*, and the competition with his mates will finally polish up his training as a *mugambi*. All Meru are, like most Africans, good speakers, but the best logician, though his oratory may not be as brilliant, is regarded by them as the best *mugambi*.

(*c*) *The lineage*.[1] The lineage is called by the same term as the clan, *mwiriga*. The lineage must be distinguished from the clan, for it is seen in action as a corporate unit, territorially as well as socially defined.

The lineage can be described as a section of clan members, bound together by actual genealogies, generally living on the same area of cultivated land. Members of the lineage are not restricted to the same territory; they can elect to cultivate in some other land of their clan. The lineage must not, however, be confused with the extended family which does not function as a distinct social unit among the Meru. Generally, in ordinary speech, the lineage is meant when the term *mwiriga* is used. Sometimes the distinction from the clan as a whole is made clear by the term *mwiriga junthe*, applied to the clan as opposed to the lineage.

Within the lineage there is one elder, a *mugambi*, who is recognized as the head and leader of the lineage. He convenes the meetings of the elders, and must always

---

[1] The term 'lineage' is here used in the anthropological sense of a line of living agnates related by actual descent from a common ancestor.

THE MERU   15

take part in all social transactions of the lineage, initiations
and other ritual ceremonies, marriage, trade or cattle
exchanges. He must be one of the senior *agambi*, but not
necessarily the most senior or the genealogical head of the
lineage. In any case he always acts as, or for, the genealogical head of the lineage.

(*d*) *Parental authority.* The family is the next unit
operating within the clan. It is based on the formula
father-mother-child which in polygynous homesteads is
complicated by a plural number of wives. Within the
family the authority of the father is paramount, but
is limited by the authority of the elders of the clan-
lineage in matters beyond the family's province. Rather
than limited, it should be said that the authority of the
father is stressed in matters regarding the family and
overlapping the family with relation to all the other elders
with whom he sits in councils, because the father is the
only person entitled to speak for the family as a whole.
He represents a corporate body, and as such he constitutes the prime root of authority. Indeed, in a
society, like the Meru, in which there was no centralized
source of authority, parental authority is the basic
principle of all forms of authority. The father derives his
status from nature and he will never lose it until death. At
the same time his status needs to be officially established,
and this is done at the time of initiation when his son is
born again into the Meru larger family. It is then that
the father becomes an elder. The elders are the fathers.
It cannot be otherwise. As such they are equal, and their
rights are equal. It is thanks to the age-class system, that
cuts across the clan and family organization, that an
official identity of status is established between all the
fathers.

The position of the elders, the position of the Mugwe,

16 THE MUGWE, A FAILING PROPHET

the comments and laments of the elders with regard to the new way of life, will be better understood if this principle of parental authority is borne in mind.

(e) *Blood-brotherhood.* There were different ways of establishing blood-brotherhood, *giciaro*. The original form, still vividly remembered, if not practised, was for the two participants to suck each other's blood. Other forms could be most extraordinary, as the one described by an Igembe elder: ' If in a fight you are about to strike at your opponent, and the spear falls from your hand, then it is God that has saved your adversary and you will be bound to him by *giciaro* '. Originally blood-brotherhood was entered into by two individuals: but as its obligations are inherited it was soon extended to clans and lineages or their sub-divisions. There were many reasons why blood-brotherhood was established: friendly, ritual, military and social. It was not limited to the Meru, but could be extended to outsiders as well. The Rendille of Marsabit, Northern Frontier, are blood-brothers of the Igembe.[1] The parties related by blood-brotherhood were pledged to be hospitable to each other, to be at peace, and to help each other in case of attack. Generally *giciaro* implied also an exogamous regulation by which members of the two clans or lineages were prohibited from marrying. It was a measure of good strategy to enter into a military blood-brotherhood, as this was done, generally, with clans or sub-tribes not bordering on each other in order to create a second front at the back of the enemy in case of war with any of the bordering neighbours. The Chuka are bound by *giciaro* with the Igembe, but not with the bordering Muthambi; they were also bound to some sections of the Tigania. The Imenti are related by

---

[1] Cf. Lambert 1950, p. 14. (See Bibliography.) See also p. 56 fn.

THE MERU 17

giciaro to the Tharaka, except the Imenti of Gitie who border on the Tharaka.

Blood-brotherhood can be terminated by a declaration to that effect ; this often happens following a mishap that cancels the original ' miracle ', or by a serious breach of the rules of the game.

4. THE AGE-SET SYSTEM

In the old Meru organization the system had a significance which it has lost today. It no longer appeals to the youth, whose interests now extend far beyond their own lineage and tribe, thanks to education, employment, trade, and wider political associations.[1] The age-set system was closely related to the office and activity of the Mugwe.

(a) *Initiation.* The time for initiation was, and still is, after a boy has reached puberty. Its main object is to train the character of the candidate and give him instruction in the lore of his people. The first and major test is on the flesh by circumcision. This now offers an opportunity for an outburst of wild excitement and dancing, lasting for a few days, which perhaps can hardly be compared with what it must have been when circumcision came as the climax of a long wait at the opening of a new period.

Soon after circumcision, the patients were sheltered in a small hut, *iganda*, where they were fed until the wound was healed.

' To be circumcised,' observed an Imenti elder, ' is nothing: even women are operated upon.[2] What matters

[1] There is no better description of the Meru ' age-set system ' than H. E. Lambert's in *Kikuyu Social and Political Institutions*, 1956, passim.

[2] Since April 1956, clitoridectomy has been officially forbidden throughout Meru.

T.M.   C

18 THE MUGWE, A FAILING PROPHET

and makes a youngster a good initiate, *muthaka*, is his self-respect and good-behaviour.'

(*b*) *The gaaru*. In order to be properly trained, the initiates were not allowed to live in the same village as their families, but had to reside in a special house, *gaaru*. The *gaaru* is indeed a training centre, and as such is to be regarded as a real social institution of the Meru. As early as 1912, A. M. Champion gave a description of the *gaaru* among the Tharaka that can be quoted here as applying literally to the *gaaru* of all the Meru:

> The unmarried men, and those whose children are not yet circumcised, cannot sleep in the villages unless they are sick. In each settlement, therefore, the young men build for themselves one hut generally hidden in a thicket close to the settlement. These huts are perfect works of art. They are about 20 to 25 feet in diameter, and from 10 to 14 feet high, and built of very stout, well fashioned poles. The doorway is about 3½ to 4 feet in height, and extends up to the level of the eave. The walls are composed of stout posts placed into the ground close together. One enters by a sort of wattle passage, which is, in reality, the close-up end of a continuous sort of wattle bedstead running completely round the whole hut; standing in the middle it gives one the impression of a circular saloon with berths all round. These huts are never occupied during the day, and I never found any sign of habitation, except fire. The care with which these huts are built and the excellence of the workmanship struck me very favourably.[1]

Nowadays *gaaru* are no longer so well built, though it was still possible to see some of the kind described among the Igembe only a few years ago. An ordinary,

---

[1] Champion, 1912, p. 74, cf. Dundas, 1915, p. 237–38 : ' In Theraka the warriors live in batches of about thirty in one hut, each hut being governed by the senior warrior, who in time of war commanded them under the *kithoga*.' (See Bibliography.)

THE MERU

larger hut is at present used as *gaaru*. Even this is another indication of different interests on the part of Meru youth: the best of them are at school.

Gaaru ni ya nthaka cia mwiriga, ' the *gaaru* is for the initiates of the lineage '. It was, therefore, a territorial and social unit reflecting the extension of the lineage. Among the Tharaka the link between the lineage and the *gaaru* is so stressed that the term *gaaru* is frequently taken to mean *mwiriga*—lineage. Where a lineage had only a few initiates they could join those of a neighbouring lineage. During the period in the *gaaru* they were visited by their sponsors and also by the Mugwe. No girl was allowed near the *gaaru*. Each initiate was given in turn a sheep by his father or sponsor to eat with his fellow inmates. The occasion was called *murano/mirano*. In the same manner they were given a bull which they ate in some valley or in the bush, and the occasion was called *renta*. The main purpose, however, of their being in the *gaaru*, was educational and military. The visits of the elders and of the Mugwe were occasions for instruction, good manners, and respect for the elders, sexual matters and moral virtues being the main subjects. The secrecy of much of this information was strongly impressed upon them. The initiates were also looked after by the senior initiates who could even beat them to improve their behaviour and manners. Such beatings were common, and came to be regarded as a normal part of the training. From a military point of view the *gaaru* was like a period of conscription, and the young initiates formed a standing army for the defence of the country. Their military activity, however, was not restricted to defensive exercises only. At frequent intervals the *nthaka* were allowed to organize raids against neighbouring tribes or sub-tribes, though not without the blessing of the Mugwe. Raiding

20 THE MUGWE, A FAILING PROPHET

cattle was considered a normal part of the training, and the initiates regarded it as a means of enhancing their own prestige and fame.

The initiates had their inner council: in Imenti, Igembe Tigania and Tharaka, it was called *kiama kia Ramare* (Igembe and Tigania, *Lamalle*); in Chuka, Muthambi, *njuri ya gaaru*.

Life in the *gaaru* continued until the initiates were allowed to marry. Before doing so they had first to be initiated into *kiama kia Nkomango*, 'the council of the throwing stone', the initiation consisting of a number of very degrading ordeals, so repulsive that it has been consistently opposed by all Christian and educated Meru. Permission for the whole group to marry was formally given by a blessing of the Mugwe.

(*c*) *The formation of the age-classes*. The disruption that has taken place since the cessation of warriors' activity, has made it very difficult to obtain a description of the system as it worked when it was fully observed. Moreover, one tends to apply to the succession of the age-classes formed according to a natural seasonal calendar, the precision of the western calendar, with baffling results. One point which is particularly difficult to determine is the lists of age-classes that may be dictated by the elders. Among all the Meru sub-tribes I collected a number of such lists: in only one case, among the Imenti, I was surprised to discover that one of them corresponded almost exactly to a similar list recorded by Mr. W. H. Laughton in 1938 and published by Lambert. One must realize, however, that the order of names may be immaterial, the important point being to know the working of the system and its value in the structure of Meru society. I shall now try to describe the system, as I

THE MERU 21

have come to know it from my Meru informants, as simply and clearly as possible.

The initiates of a single circumcision period were first organized into a special age-set or age-unit. An interval of some years (in recent years it has been four years or seven–eight seasons), was allowed to elapse before another circumcision period was opened. During the closed period no circumcision was to take place, all attention being given to the training of the newly initiated. An open period could last one year or more (two or three seasons), according to the number of candidates. The length of the periods was dictated primarily by the physical development of the candidates. The age units were generally three and they had fixed names to which could be added an occasional individual name. The three age-units were finally formed into an age-class after a period from the formation of the first age-unit, of about fifteen years. The formation of the age-class took place during a time when the great ceremony *ntuiko* was celebrated throughout the country. All the age-classes were under an alternating dual division. The names of these divisions were *Thathi*, *Ntiba*, among the Chuka; *Kiruka*, *Ntiba*, among the other Meru.

Alternating Division 1.   *Alternating Division 2.*

Age-Unit 1			Age-Unit 1		
Age-Unit 2	} AGE-CLASS 1		Age-Unit 2	} AGE-CLASS 2	
Age-Unit 3			Age-Unit 3		

Age-Unit 1			Age-Unit 1		
Age-Unit 2	} AGE-CLASS 3		Age-Unit 2	} AGE-CLASS 4	
Age-Unit 3			Age-Unit 3		

The old system in its exact form and time-rhythms of closed and opened periods is still observed among the

22 THE MUGWE, A FAILING PROPHET

Igembe and the Tigania, where the names of the three age-units are: *Ndinguri, Kobia, Kaberia*. Among the Imenti and the other sub-tribes initiation can now take place every year and there are cases, though still rare, of boys who prefer to be circumcised at the hospital rather than follow the old system. The Tharaka have been singled out by some writers as differing from the other Meru for their uninstitutionalized age-set system. My evidence shows that their system was structured, as among the other Meru sub-tribes, with minor differences as are to be found everywhere. We have quoted the description of the Tharaka *gaaru* by Champion, an institution that tallies exactly with that obtaining with the other sub-tribes. The three age-units were formed into an age-class, as among the other sub-tribes, at a ceremony called *rukunyi* not dissimilar to the *ntuiko*.

(*d*) *The ntuiko*. The ceremonial of the *ntuiko* (a word which means break) was, and still is, the occasion for the handing over, or breaking, the authority of an age-class, generally called the ruling age-class, to the next following age-class. The latter is thus formally and first recognized as an age-class.

As is apparent from the diagram above, the handing-over takes place between one alternating division and the other, so that the age-class in power is always of the opposite alternating division from the next preceding and the next following age-class in power.

The nature of the authority or power handed over needs clarifying. In Meru society authority, as already noted, rests entirely on the elders, all the elders of all the age-classes. The only differentiation between them is by seniority, which is officially defined at this very ceremony, the *ntuiko*. Authority as a basic right, therefore, cannot

THE MERU 23

be handed over by the elders. What the new age-class receives is a kind of delegated power by which its members are expected to assume a primary and thorough control of things communal. The ritual *ntuiko* modifies the opposition of the old retiring age-class towards the new one. The age-class in power should be called the ' managing ' rather than the ' ruling ' age-class. Their power does not entirely exclude the elders of the other age-classes. These can always take part in councils if the matter discussed is in their interest and concerns them and their opinion, especially if one happens to be a distinguished *mugambi* or a very old man, may be as deciding a factor as that of a member of the age-class in power.[1] Thus authority, among the Meru, does not take the form of a monopolistic bureaucracy, but of a distributive democracy or gerontocracy.

The actual ritual of *ntuiko* is intimately connected with the office of the Mugwe. We shall, therefore, postpone its description to a later stage. The Mwimbi, Muthambi, etc., are described by the other Meru elders as performing a *ntuiko* ceremony differently. Some Chuka said that those sub-tribes ' kill a man ' at their *ntuiko*. The rite, if it ever existed, has not been practised in recent times, nor are the present Mwimbi prepared to admit the truth of the statement even for the past. The point is important because it offers more evidence of the peculiar position of the Mwimbi group among the Meru. The *ntuiko* ritual covers a long period during which all the country is happily feasting; the elders of the retiring age-class are at liberty, during that period, to do whatever they like; thus one

---

[1] ' In the untouched system the differentiation between the ruling sets and the rest was of more relevance to participation in ritual than in tribal decisions.' Lambert, 1956, p. 135. (See Bibliography.) This is also the reason why shrewd men, though not of the ruling age-class, could always prevail and practically run the country, whatever the age-class in power.

24 THE MUGWE, A FAILING PROPHET

sees them (or hears of them) going around spending time at drinking parties or indulging in the sort of behaviour that would be considered shameful at any other time.

At a special ceremony the new age-class is blessed and given a name: both functions are a privilege of the Mugwe.[1] Among the Meru to be given a name is a qualification of great consequence: it signifies an acknowledgement, a consecration of one's status in the eyes of society. Every Meru is given a number of names at different stages of his life.[2] So, at the *ntuiko* the age-class comes to life as an organized body, and its status in the structure of Meru society is fully accepted and consecrated. After this, the age-class is fit to take over management of general matters.

5. THE *NJURI* ASSOCIATION

It is within the structure of the age-class system that the association of the *njuri* has been formed. It is, as already stated, an indigenous unit of government, which has been recently incorporated into the African District Council.

The association with its full hold on social and political life still survives among the Igembe and the Tigania. Among the Imenti and the Tharaka, its inner organization and force have become much looser. In Chuka and Mwimbi the association has been somewhat in abeyance. There is evidence showing that the *njuri* association is a relatively

---

[1] Lambert, 1956, p. 47, speaking of the Embu writes: 'It appears that the choice of the names for the generations at the various stages rests with one family of the Igamuturi clan, who are said also to exercise a general direction of the whole proceeding. No doubt we can see in this, as also in the account of the Kikuyu handing-over, some hereditary function vested in a kinship group or groups, rather like the *ugwe* of the Meru.'

[2] In modern times, and especially during the Emergency, this has been a cause of embarrassment. It is very difficult to make the young Meru understand that they should keep one name only and stick to it for good, if they want to avoid petty annoyances with all the cards and passes they have to carry at present.

THE MERU

recent institution which has skilfully succeeded in super-
seding the traditional inner councils of the elders. While
some Chuka elders state that the *njuri* were not indigenous
to them, in Igembe I was told that the *njuri* had stolen
batunyire, the authority of 'the commanders,' *kiama kia
wathi*, i.e. of the council of elders in charge of legis-
lation.[1]

Members of the *njuri* association are selected elders who
have passed through a series of special initiation rites and
paid the established fees. One becomes a member by
invitation from the senior members. For all practical
purposes the choice of an elder for *njuri* membership
depends entirely on the inviting members, which shows
that, though all the elders are eligible, not all of them
may be asked to join. The choice generally falls on elders
who have distinguished themselves by their brilliance and
their wealth. Indeed, wealth, among the Igembe, is a
conditio sine qua non for two reasons: first, a wealthy man
wields greater influence in the community; second, only
a wealthy man can afford to pay the exorbitant entrance
fees.

In April 1955, I calculated the total fees required by the
Igembe *njuri* from a newly associated member at different
stages of his initiation. It amounted, in rams, goats, firewood, indigenous beer, at current market prices, to
rather more than one thousand shillings. However, among
the other sub-tribes the entrance fees are very low, about
fifteen shillings.

The first prerequisite for eligibility to the association
is normally initiation into *kiama kia Nkomango*. Among
the Igembe this initiation is preceded by *gutumerua ota*: an

---

[1] At Mutuate, Daniele M. Mugami wa M. Ngiceu, an elder of the age-
class *Micubu*, told me that at the time of his grandfather, Mwenda Thakimbu
of the age-class *Gwantai*, the *njuri* did not have power in Igembe.

26 THE MUGWE, A FAILING PROPHET

initiation to ' wisdom '. Such a prerequisite was obvious in the old system, but since educated Meru have refused it, its mere existence has become a controversial subject.

The next stage is *njuri nceke*, who are the elders entitled to take part in the general assemblies of all the *njuri*, which are convened at Nceke, a plain between the Upper Imenti Forest and the first slopes of the Nyambene Range in the country of the Tigania.

The stage above is formed by the *njuri mpingire*, who are said to be the *agambi* of the *njuri*, the most eminent of them all : as such they are also called *ariki/mwariki*, i.e. those who reached the end, the top.

Among the Tharaka the three stages have corresponding names : *kiama kia nkome, kiama kiiru* or *mbiru*, and *kiama rwamba*.

The *njuri* elders have so much strengthened their control of general matters that they have become the real masters of the country. The highest grade has authority to pass sentence of death. Being an inner association grafted on to the larger age-class organization, they have distinguished themselves by their secrecy, so much so that they have sometimes been regarded as a secret society. There is no doubt that the restricted number of elders who become members of the association has made this a closed circle. Moreover, the very high power possessed by the *njuri*, against which there is no possible appeal, makes their membership a sort of privilege, open to abuses. It is a common experience to hear complaints levelled against the *njuri:* ' the power of the *njuri* is for their own good: if one wants to be *njuri* it is only for his own benefit not for the good of all.' [1]

Such criticisms have increased during recent years and

---

[1] *Unene bwa njuri ni gwicua muntu wega bwawe; muntu eenda kuaa njuri, i wega bwawe acuaga, ti wega bwa antu bonthe.*

have been made particularly by Christian Meru, in connection with the attempt of the Administration to reform and modernize the *njuri* association in order to make it an instrument of government. A major obstacle to the aim of the Administration has been the refusal of all educated Meru, who are almost all Christian, to be initiated as *njuri*. An attempt has been made to overcome the difficulty by establishing a Christian oath, as a form of initiation. It was agreed to consider membership of a Christian church as an equivalent to the initiation into *kiama kia Nkomango*, and a number of Christian elders were thus co-opted into the association. It soon became clear, however, that the Christian *njuri* were only considered *nuthu njuri*, half *njuri*. In 1955, when the Administration called the *njuri* to be members of the African District Council, efforts were renewed to convince the *njuri* to accept the Christian initiation as valid. The attempt seems to have been a success among the Imenti where a very great number of Christians were initiated. It was, for all practical purposes, a failure with the Igembe where the *njuri* were not willing to accept any other form of initiation except the old one.

The attempts to reform the *njuri* and make them a suitable body for modern government are certainly to be considered with the greatest interest. But the analysis of the position of the *njuri* association, especially in the old structure of Meru society, leaves the unbiased investigator uncertain on the problem. If authority, as it seems, rests basically with the elders, then the *njuri* should be considered as a superstructure of closed councils open only to a few. As such they are not ' constitutional ', so to speak. It is, therefore, evident why the recent inclusion of the *njuri* by the African District Council should have caused so much concern among those elders who either

28 THE MUGWE, A FAILING PROPHET

refused, or were not invited, to become members of the association.

6. CHANGING AGENCIES

The Mau Mau emergency has called for a more efficient expansion of the administrative organization. Before that, the few District Officers attached to the administration all resided in Meru Town, and used to visit the District occasionally as routine and special needs required. The staff of Officers has now been greatly increased, and they have taken up residence among the various sub-tribes at the Division and Location headquarters. Their mere presence is having a great effect on the people. Sub-tribes, like the Tharaka or the Igembe, who had for long been left to fend for themselves, look now with confidence to the Administration as something personal, real and effective. The new situation has also enhanced the authority of the chiefs and headmen, who are now chosen from among educated Meru. All the country is covered by karanis, agricultural assistants, and other civil servants.

Practically all the educational work in Meru has been carried on by the Missions. There are three Protestant Churches doing missionary work: the Presbyterian Church of East Africa among the Mwimbi and the Chuka; the Methodist Church in Imenti, Igembe, Tigania and Tharaka; and the Seventh Day Adventist Church in Tharaka. The Catholic Church, represented by the Consolata Fathers, has worked in the area since 1913 and has established Missions among all the Meru sub-tribes.

In 1957 the number of schools and pupils was as follows :

		Schools	Pupils
District Education Board:	Primaries	1	280
	Intermediates	1	33
Presbyterian Church:	Primaries	31	4,536
	Intermediates	6	814
Methodist Church:	Primaries	45	7,077
	Intermediates	7	814
Catholic Church:	Primaries	79	9,264
	Intermediates	7	782
TOTALS		177	23,600

There are also two Secondary Schools, one Government at Meru Town, the other Catholic at Nkubu, Nkuene Location.

The work of the Missions for the education, both religious and civic, of the Meru has been considerable. The number of Christians is still low, but though they constitute a minority of the total population, they form, as a social group, the most progressive section of the District, ' enough to leaven the whole batch '.[1]

[1] Matt. XIII, 33.

Chapter Two

VISITING THE AGWE

It was essential for my work to establish personal contact with each one of the Agwe. This took me all around the country of the Meru sub-tribes, where I was able to visit and interview every Mugwe in his own house and among his own people. Though they were always co-operative, I did not expect from their information the solution of all the problems that their presence raises for the anthropologist. In some cases, as if unwilling to commit themselves, they were growing reticent. The situation among the Imenti is peculiar, as I shall describe below, and it was among them that I found it a most exacting task to put together all the evidence in a way that would make sense. My interview extended to a very great number of elders of all ages, as a necessary source and a control for the comparative use of all the information.

I. THE PROPHET AND THE DIVINER IN IGEMBE

The visitor who first enquires about the Mugwe in Igembe is left uncertain of the situation because he may be given information which sounds contradictory and varies from place to place. The reason is that there are two men in Igembe, both called Mugwe, and both objects of the same respect as one might expect with relation to such personages. Later on one discovers that the information given is not incorrect, but that the two men represent two quite distinct institutions: one is the Mugwe

32 THE MUGWE, A FAILING PROPHET

proper; the other is a visionary diviner or *kiruria*, who is also commonly called the Mugwe.

(a) *The Mugwe Proper*

Antubociu, a place about seven miles east of Maua Market, Maua Location, Nyambene Division, is the residence of the present Mugwe. The place can also be referred to as Ancenge, from the name of the clan of its inhabitants.

The Mugwe is called by his personal name, M. Mugambi Baituuru. His clan and lineage is Ncenge. He is not a very old man, his age-class being Ithalie. The power of the Ugwe has always been retained by his family. The list of past Agwe reckons fifteen names, as follows, and it is said that the list goes back to the very first Mugwe:

1.	Iguru	2.	M. Iguru
3.	Tai	4.	Mbiti
5.	Gakulu	6.	Baibwamba
7.	Thabwari	8.	Thakairi
9.	Baithiami	10.	M. Ikurui
11.	King'ang'a	12.	Baikunywa
13.	Baituuru	14.	Muruku
15.	M. Mugambi		

The authority of the Mugwe is described by M. Mugambi, and also by all the Igembe, as the greatest. His election is closely connected with the formation of the age-class, and takes place at the *ntuiko*. Among the Igembe the Mugwe does not hold office for life, but his power lasts for the time the age-class that has seen his appointment remains in power. It is the age-class, in the words of the Igembe, that ' generates ' him. Thus M. Mugambi is the Mugwe of the age-class Ratania. Muruku was the Mugwe for the age-class Micubu. It is relevant to report

VISITING THE AGWE 33

here the cycle of the Igembe age-classes, as I collected them from the Mugwe and the other elders:

NTIBA: alternating division 1.   *KIRUKA: alternating division* 2.

1.	Micubu	2.	Ratanya
3.	Lubetaa	4.	Miriti
5.	Gwantai	6.	Gicungi
7.	Kiramunya	8.	Ithalie
9.	Micubu	10.	Ratanya

M. Mugambi, the Mugwe for Ratanya, is himself a member of the Ithalie age-class. Muruku, the Mugwe for Micubu, is himself of Kiramunya age-class. The structural distance between them should be noted as it is not without significance. It should also be noted how the election of the Mugwe follows the two alternating divisions.

When, at the next *ntuiko* ceremonial, the old Mugwe retires as Mugwe, he may still continue to bear the title of Mugwe, but it is a name of honour, void of power, for all the power belongs now to the new Mugwe. The position of the retired Mugwe is that of a highly respected elder.

Apparently, there should be one Mugwe for each one of the age-classes. It seems, however, that this rule is not strictly observed, as Muruku was the Mugwe for two following age-classes.

(b) *The Diviner*

M. Lunyiru M. Ithiria is his name. His clan is Ntune; his age-class Kiramunya. The place where he lives is called Mumarui and it is not far beyond Kangeta Market on the road to Maua.

His welcome to our party (there was also the Father in charge of Tuuru Mission and my assistants) was friendly and, I should say, of a style that befits a diviner who is said to have visions from God. His house is on the

34   THE MUGWE, A FAILING PROPHET

lower slopes of a hill, covered by a thicket of high canes. On our approach he came out of the thicket, and, lifting his arms high to the sky, he greeted us, calling on God in the great Masai way: *Ngai ai, Ngai ai,* 'My God, my God.' I took up the phrase and answered '*Ngai*' at each of his invocations and he continued with evident satisfaction.

The effect of the brief litany was immediate and a pleasant atmosphere of friendship was soon established.

He welcomed all my questions eagerly and his answers were to the point. I could not help remarking how surprised I was at his warm reception, to which he answered that he was merely respecting the instructions of his father M. Ithiria. M. Ithiria was also a Mugwe of the same order as M. Lunyiru. He had foretold the arrival of the white men, dictating that they were to be welcomed: ' Red strangers will come to you. Do not do any harm to them, but lift your arms to them (in welcome). If they ask for something we shall give it to them. No one must resent that. Such is what God tells us .'[1]

M. Lunyiru stated that there is no contradiction between his work and that of the Mugwe of Antubociu, but that his own work is entirely of God: *ngugi yakwa ni ngugi ya Murungu,* ' my work is the work of God'. M. Lunyiru has no relation whatsoever with the age-classes and their formation. This distinguishes his office from that of the Mugwe proper. Moreover, though his father was also a diviner, M. Lunyiru did not get his call as an hereditary succession, but directly from God.

Women used to go in long procession to consult M. Lunyiru. The difference between the Mugwe proper and

---

[1] *Ngua ntune ikeja kiri bui, bugatonga: tamburukieni njara. Beetia gintu, tubanenkere. Guti we akathura. Buria Ngai atuiraga.*—Two days after our visit, M. Lunyiru went to Tuuru Mission and he offered to the Father in charge, Rev. Fr. Soldati, two sugar-canes in return for our visit to him.

the diviner is greatly stressed by the elders: ' that man of Antubociu is greater than all the others, because he knows better than they all .'

2. THE MUGWE AND THE MUKIAMA OF THE TIGANIA

In Tigania the office of the Mugwe obtains among the Igoki-Urio division. Among the Athwana-Umotho division it is paralleled by the office of the Mukiama. The elders state that there is no difference between the two offices, except for territories. In conversation with the elders, sometimes spontaneously, at others at my request, the question arose as to which of the two officers was greater in status. Opinions were not consistent. The evidence, however, seems to be in favour of the Mugwe of the Igoki division. Chief Bartholomew M. Igweta of Kianjai Location, an intelligent and energetic elder, stated that the Mugwe was for all the Tigania, and the Mukiama for some age-units only. This is certainly no longer so, but the statement, which came from a member of the Mukiama's division, may be taken as an indication of a different situation in the past. It seems probable that the Mukiama was an assistant of the Mugwe proper, or a minor Mugwe, who succeeded in imposing his authority over the Athwana section.

A further point of difference between the Igoki and the Athwana divisions is to be found in the formation of the age-classes. There seems to be some dislocation with the Athwana. In fact, while the Igoki were celebrating their *ntuiko* at the end of 1956 and the beginning of 1957, and a new Mugwe took office forming the Ratanya into an age-class, the Athwana remained static, and they will wait until 1958 for their time to mature. The present Mugwe of the Igoki is the head of the Ratanya age-class; the

36   THE MUGWE, A FAILING PROPHET

present Mukiama of the Athwana is the head of the
Itharia.

The following is the cycle of the age-classes as I collected it (A) in Mikinduri Location (Igoki), and (B) in
Kianjai Location (Athwana).

A. *NTIBA: alternating division* 1.   *KIRUKA: alternating division* 2.

1. Ntangi	2. Mbaine
3. Likinju	4. Ratanya
5. Lubetaa	6. Miriti
7. Gwantai	8. Gicungi
9. Murungi (Kiramunya)	10. Itharie
11. Micubu	12. Ratanya

B. *NTIBA: alternating division* 1.   *KIRUKA: alternating division* 2.

1. Lubetaa	2. Miriti
3. Gwantai	4. Gicungi
5. Kubai	6. Itharie
7. Micubu	8. Ratanya

(a) *The Mugwe of Igoki*

At the time of my first visit in 1955, the Mugwe was
M. Ikwenga M. Ithaing'u. His clan was Ntune; his age-
class Murungi. He lived at Kigucwa, a place off the main
road to Maua about three miles from Mikinduri Market.
I went to see him personally, but my first contact was
only through intermediaries, and he remained inside
his house. Finally, having satisfied himself as to my
credentials, he appeared in full regalia, the staff of office
in his hand and followed by a retinue of elders around
whom gathered a throng of curious people from the
nearby huts. He has now retired from office to make
way for the next Mugwe. At my second visit, he was no
longer in authority and he had no objection to my speaking
to him directly as an ordinary common man. This time

VISITING THE AGWE 37

he was living in a temporary shelter in the middle of a sugar-cane plantation, on the other side of the main road.

The present Mugwe is called *M. Kiremi M. Mbuguri*. He is of the same lineage and clan, Ntune, as his predecessor. When I first met him, he was sitting in council with the elders, in the traditional attire of the Tigania elders: a goat skin around his loins, a staff, and a skin crown on his head. The council were sitting in a rocky place in a corner of a large plain. As with the Mugwe of the Igembe, the election and retirement of the Mugwe is closely related to the formation of the age-classes, and hence with the alternating divisions of the age-system. M. Ikwenga is himself a member of the age-class Murungi, and held office as leader of Micubu. M. Kirimi is of the Itharie age-class and he is the Mugwe for Ratanya.

(b) *The Mukiama of the Athwana*

In the Meru language the term *mukiama* can be applied to anyone who is a member of a council, *kiama*. (The term can also be pronounced by the Tigania as *mukyima*, with no difference of meaning.) It is only among the Athwana Tigania that the word indicates an office of such great distinction as that of the Mugwe.

The present Mukiama is *M. Itumbiri Mucung'a*. His clan is Andoni; and his residence is to be found at Muruuta, on the left side of the road to Kangeta, where it branches off to Tigania Catholic Mission.

The Mukiama of Kubai age-classs was M. Kula.

M. Itumbiri, as already stated, describes himself as the chief, *munene*, of the Itharie age-class, though his own age-class is Gicungi. He performed the ceremony of blessing for this, but at the next he will leave office for another Mukiama, who is already indicated in the person of M. Igwatho, of the same lineage as M. Itumbiri. The

38 THE MUGWE, A FAILING PROPHET

evidence seems to indicate that for the Mukiama the succession from within the same lineage is not consistently observed.

3. THE SITUATION AND THE RESIDENCE OF THE IMENTI MUGWE

The residence of the Mugwe of the Imenti is at Kirirwa, Lower Abothoguci Location, a place which is now cut across by a side road to Kaongo Market. Incidentally, the opening of this road is vividly remembered by the elders of the Imenti. They recollect with awe the strange events that took place when the work reached the Mugwe's residence. A great storm suddenly developed; trees fell down from both sides of the track, until the Mugwe came out to reassure the workers because ' it was not their fault that they were taking the road through his place, a place that was of his own and of nobody else'. As they were not guilty, he blessed them ('was he not their father, even their God, indeed a very good man? '), and so they were able to continue their work.

The clan of the Imenti Mugwe is Umu.

The situation among the Imenti is rather unusual. From all the information I collected, one main conclusion may be drawn, namely, that the office of the Mugwe is at present somehow in abeyance. In 1953-54 the age-class Kiruja was formed; the *ntuiko* was celebrated but there was no blessing by the Mugwe nor any other ritual in connection with his office. The power of the Mugwe is summarized by the elders in the power of holding *kiragu*. We shall see, later on, the full meaning and implications of this word. *Kiragu* is now held by M. Ngitira M. Athongu, who lives at Kirirwa. It is said that for some time *kiragu* had been entrusted to a very old woman, *mwekuru ntindiri*, of the Mugwe's family who, being

VISITING THE AGWE

ntindiri, i.e. beyond the age of childbearing, was thought to be free from sin and holy.[1]

The only reason which is openly stated to be the cause of the present state of affairs with regard to the Mugwe of the Imenti is the new way of life: *gitumi ni Comba iji,* ' the cause is this new (European) way of life'. And more explicitly: *Aconko bakwija, guti bendire kajukia (kiragu), gitumi ni kwaga kaana ga kujukia,* ' when the Europeans came, there was no one who wanted to take *(kiragu),* the reason being that there is no boy to take it'. From other information from elders of Nkuene Location, who had been my friends since my arrival at Nkubu Mission and were more confident, the whole situation seems to be bound up with some apparent legal impurity because of certain deaths (perhaps murders?) which occurred in the house of the Mugwe.

In spite of all this the respect and fear for the *kiragu,* the Ugwe, and the Mugwe, among all the elders, is still tremendous. In the past, age-classes were formed and blessed by the Mugwe at Kirirwa. There was no division, white or red, of clans that did not go to be blessed by the Mugwe. Even today, it seems that when the elders of the Imenti are asked for their opinion on matters of general interest, they look to Kirirwa for a lead; ' the law of the country is laid down there '.

Indeed, with regard to the extension of the Mugwe's authority we are left in no doubt by the Imenti. I can summarize the many statements made by the elders in the words of one of them, Kaboto M. Arethi of

---

[1] As regards the implication of the term ' woman ' in public life, the elders may use the term to describe their present political conditions: ' we are all *women:* the real *man* is the government '. It could possibly be that the reference to a *ntindiri* woman would only be an indirect way of referring to the Mugwe, because ' all the land being now in the hands of the government ', even the Mugwe is reduced to the status of a woman.

40   THE MUGWE, A FAILING PROPHET

Nkomari: *Utiji Mugwe ni we munene wa Ameru?* ' Don't you know that the Mugwe is the chief of the Meru and that there was no other chief? If we compare the Mugwe with the present chiefs, he is the greatest, he is the best, *ari muntu wa ma.*'

4. THE MUGWE OF THE THARAKA

The present Mugwe of the Tharaka lives at Kithakarani, a place about one mile inland, north-west of Chokarige Market. His name is *M. Ruanda M. Mwoga.* His clan is Kithuri, his age-class Nkonge. M. Ruanda is a middle-aged man with a family of two wives and five children. He is stated to have been called to be the Mugwe when he was still young, because his father did not live long.

In the past, the residence of the Mugwe was at Konguru, a place still pointed out in connection with an outstanding Mugwe of the Tharaka, Mutuampea, M. Ruanda's grandfather. Mutuampea, it is stated, is buried at Konguru. The indication of one's burial place is a distinction that is very rarely, if ever, made for any man, either among the Tharaka or among the other Meru. Mutuampea must have been a very great man if even his grave is still remembered! Indeed, the Tharaka go even further with regard to Mutuampea; they say that 'he was the chief and leader of all the Tharaka, since their exodus from Mbua', *Mutuampea are munene wa Tharaka yonthe, gitumi niwe waari mutungeria kuuma Mbwa.* However recent the migration from Mbwa, Mutuampea, the grandfather of the present Mugwe, was certainly not born at that time. The statement is a typical expression of a phenomenon of identification between the living Mugwe and the first mythological or historical founder of the tribe, of which we shall analyse other instances below.

VISITING THE AGWE 41

Konguru was left not many years ago in one of those migratory movements, still undertaken, to some extent, by the Tharaka, in search of new and more fertile land.

The past Agwe are still quite well remembered by the Tharaka elders. The following is a series I recorded from various informants:

1. Mwiga	7. Nyaga
2. Kithinthei	8. Mugaita
3. Kirura	9. Rugwire
4. Ncondo	10. Changine
5. Nduri	11. Mutuampea
6. Muthwerathi	12. Mwoga
	13. M. Ruanda

The elders, and also M. Ruanda, noted that not all the above named are the first-born sons of the previous Mugwe, though most are. The selection of a candidate for the office of Mugwe is first dictated, among the Tharaka, by a principle of hereditary descent, which, however, is frequently modified by consideration for the moral and physical requirements that make a candidate suitable to take up the ' tremendous ' distinction of the Ugwe.

I think I can discover a reference to the position of the Mugwe among the Tharaka in an early description of the Tharaka clans by C. Dundas: ' One of the clans seems to occupy a peculiar position superior to the rest on account of its descent from therein; its present leader is also a medicine-man, and thus commands considerable respect, and has the nearest approach to a traditional authority that I have met with in any of the three tribes (Akikuyu, Atheraka, and Akamba)'.[1] The special social position of the Mugwe's clan will be analysed at a later stage; we shall also study the difference between the Mugwe and a

[1] C. Dundas, 1915, pp. 238–39. (See Bibliography.)

42   THE MUGWE, A FAILING PROPHET

medicine-man; but the description of the authority and even the reference to the power of the clan over the rain, in my investigation finds no other correspondence among the Tharaka, except with the authority and the clan of the Mugwe.

The authority of the Mugwe extended over all the territory of the Tharaka, including the Thagichu beyond Tana River. A dichotomy of authority has been introduced by the dual division, Urio and Umotho. The Mugwe belongs to the Umotho division, therefore only the people of Umotho were privileged to take part in full array at his ceremonial blessings. Those of Urio were not expected to visit the Mugwe at his residence, but they were supposed to respect him and obey all his orders and instructions conveyed to them by members of the Umotho division. It seems that there was, or could be, some kind of friction between the two divisions that could also, in rare cases, take the form of criticism of the Mugwe, not directly and personally, which would not be fitting, but indirectly by criticizing members of the Mugwe's lineage. Criticisms may be taken as an indication of a traditional opposition between the two divisions. It is also in this sense that the statements by some Urio elders may be interpreted, that the Tharaka of Urio could follow the Mugwe of the Imenti. It has already been noted that the two Urio and Umotho divisions are not at present territorial.

On one of my visits to M. Ruanda, in 1955, I found him busy building his new residence. All his possessions had already been assembled on the spot but the huts had not been built, only the circle on which to dig the foundations having been drawn. But what impressed me most was a small structure, of a few poles, round, open-sided, and covered by thatching grass. The shelter was just completed and had evidently been given precedence

VISITING THE AGWE 43

over all the other buildings of the household. In shape it was similar to the shelter I had previously observed at the house of M. Kamunde, a great medicine-man of the Tharaka, and in which he used to hang his professional bag with all his medicines. M. Ruanda noticed my interest and invited me to inspect the shelter at closer quarters, a few yards from the side of the new houses. In the soil, at the centre, there were three stones in the pattern of the ordinary Meru fireplace. Set on the stones there was ' the bottle of the sacred honey ', and a small pot with the other ' sacred things ' of the Ugwe. I was not allowed to inspect these. The use of a bottle (it was a glass bottle), was not considered by M. Ruanda an unsuitable innovation in the things of the Ugwe. The honey, or better honey-beer,[1] is the most sacred thing of the Tharaka, as *kiragu* is for the Imenti. The story goes that the sacred honey was used originally by the first Mugwe, since when it has never been allowed to dry up. It is the Mugwe's duty to see that it never does. Noticing the care and the respect that M. Ruanda had shown for his sacred relics by completing first the sanctuary then his personal house, I was left with the impression that he was deeply conscious of the responsibility of his sacred trust.

5. THE MUGWE AND THE ASSISTANT AGWE OF THE CHUKA

Among the Chuka, besides the Mugwe proper, I also found some minor functionaries spread over the territory. They are also called Mugwe but are definitely under the authority of the Mugwe proper.

(a) The Mugwe proper

The present Mugwe of the Chuka is *M. Kiganka*

---

[1] The word commonly used by M. Ruanda and the elders was *uuki*, honey; only rarely they say *ncobi*, honey-beer, which is certainly a more exact term for the sort of liquid actually contained in M. Ruanda's bottle.

44   THE MUGWE, A FAILING PROPHET

M. Nkanata. He lives at Engakui in the area of Chera Village, south of Chuka Town, to which he had been forced to move during the Emergency, and I first visited him there in 1955. I returned to him frequently as I found him intelligent and helpful: in May 1956, I met him building his new house at Engakui where he had returned from Chera Village. His clan is Nkui, his age-class Miriti.

The return to the land of his fathers has given new hope to an old man, but M. Kiganka is still suffering from the tragedy that befell his house during the Emergency. His eldest son, a Christian, Pankratio Mureethi, was killed in ambush by the Mau Mau on a blind corner of the road to Chera Village. Pankratio Mureethi reported to the Police that he had been forced to take the oath, and was at that time co-operating with the government. Soon after that, another 'son' (in fact, a brother's son), also a Christian, Severino M. Atare, took to the forest and joined the terrorists, never to return home; early in January 1957, he was killed by a Police patrol. On the top of all these losses, the old house of M. Kiganka had been burnt down and completely destroyed by the Mau Mau: in the conflagration 'all the sacred things of the Ugwe' were dispersed.

M. Kiganka is strongly convinced of his power as the Mugwe. In his own words, it extends 'over all the Chuka, from the Thuci River to the Nithi River'. On more than one occasion he proudly claimed to be the 'kingi' (king) of all the Chuka. None is above him, neither the *Njuri*, nor anyone else: 'the Ugwe is his and nobody can take it from him'. His authority as the Mugwe is not affected by the alternating divisions of the age-system. It has always remained in the domain of his own family. It is, indeed, by hereditary succession that a candidate is selected to

VISITING THE AGWE

become the Mugwe, though the principle can be modified by consideration of the personal character of the candidate. The following is the list of the Agwe of the Chuka as dictated by M. Kiganka:

1.	Mukindi	7.	M. Tuathetu
2.	M. Bairumi	8.	Nkui
3.	Kinyinga	9.	Igambiti
4.	M. Ambaratu	10.	M. Akure
5.	Ruthitu	11.	M. Kanata
6.	Iga	12.	M. Kiganka

Two age-classes were 'made to come out', *waumagiririe*, by M. Kiganka which means that he blessed them at the *ntuiko* ceremonial. The traditional gathering place of all the Chuka was the very large plain where Chera Village has recently sprung up. Other places could also be selected on the indication of the Mugwe and the elders.

(b) The assistant Agwe

There are five assistant Agwe among the Chuka. They are:

1. *Mutueburu* in the area of Ithiu. His clan is Ugweni.
2. *Kiugu* in the area of Rubati. His clan is Nkui.
3. *Mwiro M. Abori Kamwere*, of Mwiro area. His clan is Nkui.
4. *M. Ameru* in the Kibingo area. His clan is Muraru.
5. *M. Athara* in the area of Magumoni. His clan is Wathini.

The position of these Agwe is that of subordinates, as 'of headmen with the chief'. M. Kiganka, and indeed also the other elders of Chuka, were very definite on this point: *mbere ni nii, na Mutueburu are rungu*, 'first it is I, and

46 THE MUGWE, A FAILING PROPHET

under me is Mutueburu '. Only by one or two Tharaka elders was I told that Mutueburu was the real Mugwe of the Chuka.

The function of the assistant Agwe was to act as local officers, in their own territory. Their allegiance to the Mugwe proper was shown by leading their people to him for the general blessings and assemblies.

6. THE DIVINER OF THE MUTHAMBI, MWIMBI, ETC.

The Muthambi, Mwimbi, Igoji and Miutini, have not and never had a Mugwe. When I first went to visit the Muthambi to study their structure and to make certain whether the institution of the Mugwe obtained among them, I was told by the elders that there was a Mugwe among the Muthambi in the past. But it soon became clear that what they had called Mugwe, was a diviner of past days. This man was called *M. Mworia* of the Ithima clan. He died a long time ago, and his place was taken by *M. Gacurwa*. The latter was powerful in his prophecy and became famous among all those sub-tribes. The Igoji still refer to M. Gacurwa with wonder. An Igoji elder expressed himself in this way: ' The Igoji, Mwimbi and Muthambi did have no Mugwe because they had another man, called M. Gacurwa, who could tell them whatever they wanted to know. They did not do anything without previously consulting him, for they knew that whatever he would tell them was the truth.' M. Gacurwa used to take tobacco, *atongera, mbaki*, in order to foretell. The warriors, *nthaka*, used to consult him before going on a raid, and he would tell them whether they would have luck or should refrain from going. Other diviners are also mentioned by the Igoji elders, but there seems to be no doubt that they were of the same order as M. Gacurwa, though they may be referred to by the term Mugwe.

VISITING THE AGWE 47

The work of M. Mworia and M. Gacurwa seems to have been similar to that of M. Lunyiru of the Igembe. It is only in this broad sense that the elders of Muthambi referred to these two diviners by the term Mugwe, and they did so in order to fulfil my expectations rather than to describe a real situation.

At the present, as far as I know, there is no diviner, *kiruria*, among these sub-tribes. The absence in itself is peculiar. The saying frequently heard, especially with regard to the Mwimbi, that they were not with the Meru when these came from Mbwa and that they were later intruders who managed to be assimilated by the Meru, seems to be confirmed by this negative peculiarity.

7. AMONG THE MBERE

The Mbere live in the north-eastern section of Embu District being limited on the Kamba side at the east, by the Tana River, and on the Tharaka side at the north by the Mutonga River. It was following the information of some Tharaka elders that I decided to visit the Mbere. In fact I was told that ' also the Mugwe of the Mbere went there from among the Tharaka after they had come from Mbwa '. I was disappointed. Among the Mbere, Mugwe is the name of a clan, not of an office or of a man. There is also a place on the Kyang'ombe hills that takes its name from the Ugwe, and that is *Ugwere*, the suffix */re* being locative.

The Mugwe clan of the Mbere, I was told by their elders, does not enjoy any special privilege nor has it any supernatural power, and it is ruled on the same pattern of councils, *kiama*, as all other clans. Similarly, the people of Ugwere do not possess any special power, and when they want to be blessed they go to the *mundu mugo*, the medicine-man. Of course, I was not satisfied with this.

48 THE MUGWE, A FAILING PROPHET

The institution of the Mugwe could well exist under another name. I tried to make clear my subject of enquiry assisted by Father Baggio who had been living with the Mbere for the last ten years and knows them intimately. It was only and always the *mundu mugo* that came to light as compared to the Mugwe of the Meru.

Lambert, speaking of the Embu, refers to the Igamuturi clan as the one ' exercising a general direction in the whole proceedings ' of forming the age-class. He likens this clan to the Ugwe of the Meru.[1] I came to the conclusion, after my enquiry among the Mbere, that as far as the Mbere are concerned this could not be substantiated.

8. SOME INDICATIVE PATTERNS

As a result of these contacts with all the present Agwe of the Meru, it is possible to draw some significant conclusions as a basis for a deeper analysis of the office of the Mugwe.

The presence of the Mugwe, as a leading dignitary, can be considered typical of the genuine Meru structure. The absence of the institution among the Mwimbi and the other small groups supplies negative evidence as to their earlier connection with the Meru.

The office of the Mugwe is very closely associated with the formation of the age-classes and the structure of the age-system. It is possible to see from this mere fact how the authority of the Mugwe could assume a definite political character, which, one may suppose, could certainly be exploited by strong personalities while in office.

In connection with the age-classes we can already distinguish two developments in the institution of the

[1] See footnote 1, page 24.

VISITING THE AGWE

Mugwe. One, in which the period of office of the Mugwe is temporary and coincides with the 'ruling' period of the age-classes, obtains among the Igembe and the Tigania. Among these sub-tribes, the taking-over of the Mugwe follows also the succession of the two alternating divisions of the age-system. This particular coincidence seems to have no special consequences for the office of the Mugwe. The other, in which the period of office of the Mugwe is not so strictly connected with the formation of the age-classes but lasts for life, obtains among the Chuka, the Tharaka, and possibly also the Imenti.

A further distinction is to be noted in connection with the stressing of the dual divisions, Urio and Umotho. They obtain in a very special way among the Tharaka and the Tigania. We see here that the office of the Mugwe is stated to be primarily for one section; that of Umotho among the Tharaka, that of Urio among the Tigania. As a consequence, the office may be accompanied or paralleled by another office of the same nature as the Mukiama among the Tigania, or by a form of controlled resentment or even acknowledgement of another Mugwe, that of Imenti, among the Tharaka.

Chapter Three

MYTHOLOGICAL ORIGINS OF THE UGWE

The special rôle that the Mugwe fills in the mythology of the Meru emphasizes the considerable importance of his office in the social structure of the Meru. The Meru are not rich in myths and legends, their trend of thought being matter-of-fact rather than speculative. Telling stories or recalling a tradition are regarded as fitting to the wisdom of an old man. ' I am not a very old man as yet ' is a common excuse that is frequently heard in Meru when one tries to find out about Meru past history or such other general subjects as the origin of the world or of man. The elders reckon it a great honour to be offered a chance to narrate and they are always pleased to be asked to do so. Of course, the narration is not based on a formalized and accepted version of the story as there is no writing to fix it, but it constitutes a creative process. As this, it varies with the individual. It may even become a true work of art. I was often surprised to find myself spellbound by the perfect acting of the gestures, the eyes, the mouth, the sound of the voice, with which the narrator was describing the deeds of his heroes or the phenomena of nature. There are always different versions of the same story, the originality of the individual narration being responsible for those variations. The variation, however, is not limited only to the external literary form of the narration, but may also be found in the amalgamation of several stories into a single one, and also in the change of the character of the story.

The subject matter of Meru traditions and stories is

52 THE MUGWE, A FAILING PROPHET

mainly concerned with the arrival of the people in their present country. It is only rarely that one hears a narrative referring to the creation which, however, is never described but simply stated as a work of God. A number of other stories refer to several 'cultural heroes' who performed great deeds for the Meru in their early history. It is these heroes that are generally superseded by the figure of the Mugwe in the creative process of narration. Indeed, of nearly all the stories that I recorded, there is a version in which the Mugwe is the main character. The fact is most significant. It is mythopoesis in the actual making. It shows how the Mugwe is exalted to such an idealized level that he is placed beyond and above any other figure of Meru lore.

I. IN THE BEGINNING

The following narrative is a co-ordinated account of the earliest times that was dictated by an elder of the Imenti. It constitutes a typical instance of mythopoetical amalgamation.

Narrator: M. Guoko M. Karundu, of the age-class Kiramana.

We lived at Mbwa, but God created us. At that time we did not cultivate, which means that we did not need to eat or to wear clothes. God created first a boy. Having created him, God asked him: 'Are you pleased now?' 'No, I am not pleased, and the reason that I am not pleased is that I do not have anyone with whom to play.' So a girl came out. They played together. (When you see a girl, you do not laugh but you are pleased in your heart: the satisfaction remains there and there is no need of more.) Then they started to play like children in the way that, as you know, they love each other. And they bore a child. And they saw that that was sweet and they went on loving each other and they loved each other a lot.

MYTHOLOGICAL ORIGINS OF THE UGWE 53

God came and said: ' Now I shall go and I shall give you food, but you will not taste of that tree.' A wise creature (*mugambi*) that crawls on the earth as a snake came and asked them: ' Don't you want to eat of those fruits? '—' No, our chief (*munene*) told us not to eat of that tree.' He rejoined: ' If you eat of those fruits you will have intelligence as he has.' So the woman climbed on the tree, picked a fruit and ate it. She picked a second one and gave it to her husband. The man refused. But the woman said: ' If you refuse, I will leave you alone.' The man on hearing that he would be left alone, took the fruit and ate it. Having eaten it, his throat-apple [Adam's apple] came out. It is since then that man has got a throat-apple.

And now God came and said: ' You knew that you should not have eaten of those fruits. Tell me, why did you eat of them? ' The man said: ' It is the snake that deceived me and I ate the fruit.' God said to the snake: ' I know that you are full of falsehood, therefore your head shall be crushed.' As for man he sent for the mole to tell (him) that all men will die and then arise. While the mole was on his way he met the hyena. The hyena asked him: ' Where are you going? ' ' It is God that sent me. He told me to go and tell man that they will die and arise.' ' No,' said the hyena, ' if you go and say so, what shall I eat? ' The mole said: ' No, I will tell them.' The hyena said: ' Do you want me to eat and swallow you as you are? ' So the mole became afraid on hearing that. He went and said: 'You will die and not arise.' And the mole returned to God and told him: ' I went, but the hyena deceived me and forced me to say: you will die and not arise.' On hearing that, God answered: ' You will now live under the earth, far away from me in heaven.' From that day the mole made a hole in the earth and he never comes out except during the night when he is not seen by man.

There were some prophets. They were allied with God, and they told us to give milk to a bull until it evacuated white dung. We did so, and when it evacuated white dung we took it to our enemies. These prophets were also told by God to

54 THE MUGWE, A FAILING PROPHET

collect dried dung from the cattle byre. For many days we collected it in heaps. Then the prophets said: 'Take the old cattle and the old sheep and the old goats and the old men that cannot walk. Take the small goats and the small sheep and the small calves that cannot walk, put them together with the old ones.' Then they returned to their home where they lived. When we were left alone, we gave fire to the dung-heaps and started gathering all our things. There was a prophet leading us; he had the *kiragu* and he was the Mugwe. (He was not of our clan but of another.) We arrived at Mbweene. The one who had the *kiragu* told a man of Igoki clan: 'Take the *kiragu*, hold it for me, so that I may go and scatter the enemies.' From that we knew that the power (*unene*) was ours, and that by holding the *kiragu*, we could wade through the water. That man scattered the enemies, returned, was given the *kiragu* and with that he struck the water which opened to let us pass. The man with the *kiragu* was leading us and crossed first. When we had passed, the water closed up again and our enemies did not find a place where to cross.

We crossed, and having crossed we arrived at a different land. In this land there was no food whatsoever, while on the other side our food had been plentiful. For that reason we continued to drink milk and eat meat from our cattle.

There was a mad woman: this one was found having almost all the seeds. This woman, as happens with madmen who may twist their clothes and sometimes they twist and soil them, had twisted and folded her clothes with soil in which there were seeds. It was thus that we started to cultivate the soil and to sow. At that time we used to move from one place to another, and therefore we left many fields with seeds without returning back to them.

Then we came to know that there were bad men (among ourselves). We started setting insidious traps. Their cattle went to the open country with ours at the time when there was grass. Our initiates (*nthaka*) took a big bull to eat and from others they extracted blood to drink. Once they were found to

MYTHOLOGICAL ORIGINS OF THE UGWE 55

have killed a bull: some of them remained in the bushland to enjoy themselves (*gitoji*) while others returned the cattle home. At home they said: 'Those who have remained there will return when the bull is found, but we do not know when.' They were given food that was plentiful. At night they went back and remained as long as their supplies lasted. But when their women went for firewood, they saw that there had been a feast (*gitoji*), and came home to report. And having reported, they said: 'Give us a cow,' but we refused. Having refused we started to fight until we repelled them completely. From that time we have never again seen them. And then the Europeans came.

The excursus of the above story covering, as it does, the whole span of Meru prehistorical times, from the creation to the arrival of the Europeans, is typical. Several elements may be distinguished in the story. (*a*) The narration of the creation and the fall is essentially biblical. I have never heard it told elsewhere in Meru, though other elders described how God had created all men equal with the same number of fingers, of limbs, the same mouth, the same number of eyes. One Tharaka elder remarked how God had been more successful in creating the cow than in creating the woman, because the cow can go without clothes without being ashamed, while the woman cannot. (*b*) The element of the mole and the hyena, by which death is passed as a final sentence on man, is a paleonegritic element. It connects the Meru to all the other cultures of Bantu Africa. (*c*) The element of the prophets (*iruria*) can be considered indigenous. They are the cultural heroes of the Meru, of whom we shall see other figures below. (*d*) The elements of the bull evacuating white dung, and the crossing of the water, are typically Meru. They are derived from the 'foundation story' of the Meru, as we shall see presently. Entirely Meru is also

56   THE MUGWE, A FAILING PROPHET

the figure of the Mugwe, the prophet who does not abandon the Meru but leads them through the water. ' *Kiragu* ' is the insignia of the power held by the Mugwe. The term is still used at present by the Imenti, and for its full significance we may refer to the description of the insignia of the Mugwe, pp. 94ff. (*e*) The first seeds being carried by a woman, who thus becomes the cause of the first soil-cultivation, is another paleonegritic element that is found among many other Bantu peoples. (*f*) The reference to the cattle raids which are put an end to by the arrival of the Europeans serves as a connection between the first times and modern history, and it integrates the narration into a completed whole.

2. THE EXODUS

The narration of the exodus of the Meru from Mbwa[1]

[1] H. E. Lambert, 1950, p. 7, writes as follows: ' The Meru themselves say that they came from the east and south-east of their present country and that their earliest tribal memory is of a period when they lived in subjection (perhaps slavery) to another people near " the great water ". This water has been variously identified as Lake Rudolf and the sea, but if the Meru statement that they entered their present country from the east is taken as correct (and Africans are much less likely to go wrong in directions than in other details of geography) Lake Rudolf may be safely ruled out. The place where the Meru lived near " the great water " is referred to as *Mbwa*, clearly the same word in origin as the Swahili *pwani*, the only difference being that the latter has the locative ending and (as is usually the case in Swahili) the *p*, affected by an original *n*, has discarded the nasalization in favour of aspiration, whereas in the Meru (possibly pre-Meru) word the more common Bantu retention of the *n* (becoming *m* before the labial, which itself becomes voiced) has occurred. This in itself is not conclusive evidence that the Meru lived near the sea, for the stem *pwa* can refer to any shore, sea-shore or lake-shore or riverside. But it seems probable that the alternative suggestion of Lake Rudolf has arisen from an inverted form of another traditional story which gives the Turkana (or, some say, the Rendille) a Meru origin, the story being that these people are the descendants of a group of uncircumcised young men who, tired of waiting for the elders to permit their long-delayed initiation, set off to the north or north-west, taking numbers of uninitiated girls with them. The story is somewhat vague and there seems to be no corroboration in the traditions of the people of the northern deserts, unless, as it is said, some Turkana admit a Meru origin. There is a tradition of affinity (possibly blood-brotherhood) with the Rendille and this may account for the uncertainty as to whether the

MYTHOLOGICAL ORIGINS OF THE UGWE 57

is the original story of the Meru, whence they trace their first consciousness as a tribe distinguished from all other peoples. There are different versions of the exodus. Some enumerate all the people of Kenya and East Africa who were said to be with the Meru crossing the water and who separated on reaching the new country. Others record only the Meru sub-tribes, or tell simply of the Meru. The main hero of the story is Komenjue, but in some versions his rôle is taken by other figures or superseded by the Mugwe. We shall limit ourselves to four versions which may be considered as typical.

i. The first version, which seems to me the most traditional form of the narrative, was dictated by an elder of the Imenti. I also recorded an almost identical version among the Tharaka.

When the Meru were at Mbwa they were put to several tests by their persecutors. They were first told to produce a sandal of leather from a skin having hair on both sides. They did what they could without success. There was Komenjue, a very good and wise man. ' What we have to do,' he said, ' is this: let us kill a bull, cut its dewlap, dry it, sew it together, and then take it to them.' They did so. But those people asked that now they should produce a bull giving white dung. We tried but we failed. It was Komenjue who suggested that the bull should be fed with diatomite (*iraa*) and also with milk so that he could

Turkana or Rendille are the descendants of the rebels.' In my evidence the direction referred to by the Meru with regard to their immigration to the present country is north, *urio*: this would leave the hypothesis of Lake Rudolf still open. The Igembe claim to have *giciaro*, blood-brotherhood with the Rendille. *Giciaro*, however, is a form of alliance that can be established at any time, for reasons quite independent of any kinship descent. There is no special evidence to support a relation between the Meru and the Turkana, except, perhaps, a similarity in the costume of Meru and Turkana married women, which is too vague to prove anything. In conclusion, unless more evidence is collected on this point, which seems unlikely, the problem remains a matter of speculation that still makes any solution uncertain. Another version of the Meru exodus, that I recorded among the Imenti, claims that it was at Lake Baringo that all the tribes divided, the Turkana, the Jaluo, the Lumbwa, and, of course, the Meru, the Kikuyu, etc.

58 THE MUGWE, A FAILING PROPHET

give white urine. So we fed the bull in that way. We waited for many days until he evacuated white dung. We took him to them and they were satisfied. And they said to us: 'What you have to do now is to forge a spear that when fixed on the ground, can reach the sky.' And that defeated even Komenjue who did not know what to do. So he advised us to leave that country. We arrived at a great water. Komenjue struck the water with his staff and the water divided. We crossed. Those who crossed during the night were called *njiru*, the black ones; those who crossed at dawn were called *ntune*, the red ones; those who crossed when the sun was up were called *njeru*, the white ones. And the water closed up again.

ii. The second version was dictated by the present chief of Muthara, Bartholomeo M. Igweta, Kianjai Location. It is a local version connected with the history of some specific clans of the Tigania. The first part of the story is similar to the first version. The people who persecuted the Meru are called *Ngua ntune*, the red clothes; and the sea is called *Eriatune*, the red sea. The main variation in the narrative starts when the Meru, having failed the third test of the spear, reached the sea.

Because they were on foot they could not cross the sea. Komenjue advised them that the only way out was to kill a young man and examine his entrails. He asked for volunteers: The first to come forward was Gaita (' the man who destroys himself '). He was followed by two others: Muthetu (' the soil ') and Akiuna (' the bellies '). Gaita was the one to be killed; Muthetu was to be his *mathenjeru* (i.e. the base for the sacrifice, the altar. *Mathenjeru*, sing. *ithenjeru*, are the leaves or anything else put under a beast to be slaughtered). Akiuna was to stand by and take his turn if nothing was revealed by Gaita (hence the name Akiuna, because all his bellies were trembling for fear).

Gaita was killed and his entrails revealed that the only man who could help the people out of their predicament was Gaita

MYTHOLOGICAL ORIGINS OF THE UGWE 59

himself. So he was sewn together, and also his staff that had been cut was glued together, and Gaita rose again. With his staff he struck the water which divided into two to let the people pass, etc.

In the above Tigania version, Komenjue plays only a secondary rôle as a *mugaa*, a diviner and a sacrificer. The main rôle is filled by Gaita and his assistants. They are the three cultural heroes of the Tigania, and the founders of three clans still existing today. Thus, Gaita is regarded as the founder of Antubaita clan; Muthetu the founder of Amuthetu clan; and Akiuna of Akiuna, or Antubakiuna, clan. These three clans are considered to be related and are said to possess special powers of praying and of cursing.[1]

iii. The next version introduces the Mugwe into the exodus narration. His rôle is secondary, but his position is that of the chief. The pattern of the story is biblical, and the Mugwe stands to Komenjue as Pharaoh to Moses. The narration runs as follows:

Komenjue was the man who had the staff. This man spoke by himself; he went by himself leaving the others, but he returned to say what he knew and what he saw. It was he who started the fighting (*gutetaga* = fighting by words). He said that he had dreamt dreams, and they were dreams of sufferings, there was nothing good in what he had seen. For that reason he had had for a long time a nightmare of having to leave that country altogether. He did not, however, want to speak with his chief the Mugwe, and therefore he kept silent. Nor was there anybody for many years willing to

---

[1] Among the Tharaka of Gatue, bordering on the Tigania, I also recorded a version in which the young man who gave himself up for the sacrifice is called Mutethia, the Helper. He was sacrificed, and his body dipped into the water that divided up. When all the people had crossed, Mutethia arose. I also recorded, always among the Tharaka, other traditions referring to the founders of clans, and they take their start from the exodus from Mbwa. With Mutethia there were Mukanyaki and Mukithiriini, two brothers from the same mother and they became, respectively, the heads of the Kagunda, Kamanyaki and Kithiriini clans.

60 THE MUGWE, A FAILING PROPHET

report his problem (*ontu bwawe*) to the Mugwe. What he wanted was to lead his people out of the country, and at the time he was loved more than his chief, the Mugwe. Even now the Mugwe does not want to be told by the others what he does not like to do. Etc. . . .

The last remark about the Mugwe refers to the privileges of the Mugwe: even now he cannot be asked to work as any other of the commoner Meru.

iv. The fourth version is distinguished by having the Mugwe as the main hero of the story. Komenjue disappears entirely from the scene. This version was recorded in several forms among the Imenti and the Tharaka. M. Kaboto, an Imenti elder, dictated the most elaborate form.

The Mugwe advises the people on how to solve the tests put to them by their persecutors. At the end, having failed to forge the spear that could reach the sky, ' we went to the Mugwe and asked him: ' What shall we do? ' And he replied: ' Let us go away because there is nothing else to do.' And he said: ' First select all the old cattle, and then all the old people, men and women, those who are *ntindiri* (i.e. very old, past all generating capacity), because they cannot walk. Now, in order that they may not suffer, collect as much dried cattle dung as possible so that they can use it for fire.' Now we did so and selected the old cattle and the *ntindiri* men and women, but we also selected the lambs, and the small goats, which we left for them there. So we left them there, and having lighted the fire, we started our journey until we reached the sea. But our enemies, having seen that we had started our journey, followed us and they reached us because we had refrained from crossing the sea. And when they arrived they wanted to hold the Mugwe and force him to return with them. But we understood their intentions, and as we did not know what to do, we asked what they wanted. They said: ' We want to see your chief and tell him to let you cross the sea.' Now we tried to

MYTHOLOGICAL ORIGINS OF THE UGWE   61

hide him from them. But they saw him and praised him saying that he had the power of doing all things. At that time the Mugwe was in front of us searching the water to find a place to cross. They came near him, and greeted him: 'How are you, *munene?*' He answered: 'I am looking after my people to see where they can cross.' Now they said: 'Let your people cross so that we may see where they cross, or have you not got the power of making them cross?' He rejoined: 'I have not got the power of my own, but they will cross by the power of the Mugwe.' Now they asked again: 'Where is this man called Mugwe?' He answered: 'He is behind and not yet arrived.' They started then to despise him for they wanted to kill him. But those who were present were wise enough and they did not want their chief to be touched. Now those people (the enemies) had been told that our chief had the *kiragu:* it was this *kiragu* that they wanted to catch, nothing else. They fought and they tried to strike him on that hand which holds the *kiragu;* that hand was the left hand. They aimed at that hand because it was said to hold the power of the Mugwe, but they failed. The reason that they failed was that the Mugwe had his power which is the power of God. While they were there, one of their men went into the water and he was drowned. The others were frightened and there was nothing that they could do. The Mugwe was then set free, and he saw that those people were now troubling each other, and he said: 'Now, only *Mwene inya*, God ['The owner of force,' i.e., Almighty God], knows what he will do; as for us there is nothing to do; he alone will take care of his people.' He prayed: 'Alas, One Body and Possessor of strength, give me your help, that I may lead this people of thine free from all their sufferings. Listen to my wish and to that of your children who respect Thee.' And now, he struck the water with his staff, and he saw the water dividing into two. He saw dried earth and he knew that there was a passage to cross. All crossed and it was then that he saw us through here.

Some comments readily suggest themselves on reading

62   THE MUGWE, A FAILING PROPHET

the above narrative. All the elements that we shall have to consider as constituting the institution of Mugwe are found in it. The Mugwe occupies a very special position, quite different from that of Komenjue whom he superseded. He is not only the wise man who is approached for solving the problems that face his people, he is the chief, *munene*. As chief he is protected by his own people from the attacks of his enemies. The theme of the enemies trying to kill the Mugwe is an entirely new one; new also is the theme of the people trying to conceal the Mugwe in order to save him. The power of the Mugwe resides in the *kiragu*, and it is derived from God's power. The power of the Mugwe is somehow distinguished from the person who holds the office, a distinction which shows how that power has a deeper significance for the Meru than anything personal, as for instance the power of a practitioner. The final prayer of the Mugwe to God stresses his relationship to the divinity and his peculiar relationship to what he calls first ' my people ' and then ' God's children '. The Mugwe, in this narration, is thus a wise man, a man of God, the chief, leader and saviour of his own people, holding a very special power symbolized by the *kiragu*.

3. SOME CULTURAL HEROES OF THE MERU

Komenjue, the Mugwe, Gaita, Muthetu, Akiuna, Mutethia, Mukagunda, Mukanyaki, Mukithiriini, are all figures of cultural heroes, more or less connected with the crossing of the water and the first settlement of the Meru in their present country. Some of them, like Komenjue and the Mugwe, afford a general interest for the Meru as a whole. They are described as having been the leaders of the people. All the others have a local character and are related to some definite clan rather than to all the Meru. There are other heroes of this second type among

MYTHOLOGICAL ORIGINS OF THE UGWE 63

all the Meru sub-tribes. They are not connected with the origins of the Meru, but they are remembered for great deeds, by which they saved their people or distinguished themselves from common men. All these stand in a special relation to the Mugwe. We find here the same mythopoetical phenomenon that we noticed in relation to the story of the exodus when the Meru became a single nation. The Mugwe tends to supersede all the cultural heroes and to take the rôle of *the* cultural hero par excellence. This is especially true of the first Mugwe, of whom we shall speak in the next paragraph.

Among the people of Gatue, the north-western section of the Tharaka, I recorded the following statement:

Among the Tharaka long ago, but not very long ago, there were extraordinary men, *antu ba kurigaria*. The extraordinary thing about them was this: they were not born like the other men. (*a*) In the land of Gatue a man was born, called Iboka. This man from his birth was never seen by any other man except his parents. He ended his life after one month by throwing himself into the rapids, called Kiboka, where all the people go to pray, but not all of them, only the elders. (*b*) A man, without a name, was born with teeth as if he were six or seven years old. His parents threw him to the hyenas but supplied him with all the arms of war. When the hyenas came, he killed them all, eating all the meat. When he grew into a man, he became a diviner, *kiruria*, and if he told a man something, that thing would come true. (*c*) And now, we shall listen to the wonders of another man called Mugwe. He is the man from Chokarige and he is there even now. This man is feared by all the Tharaka, from Chokarige to Gatue, and the reason why he is feared is that he was not born like other men for in his body he has a tail like an animal. . . .

From this we know that the Mugwe is among the ' men of wonders ' *antu ba kurigaria*, because he is not born like all

64 THE MUGWE, A FAILING PROPHET

the others. Further below we shall see how widespread is
the belief in the tail of the Mugwe. Let us first listen to the
full story of Iboka, because in other versions of the story
he will be somehow related to the Mugwe. The following
version was dictated by M. Remberia.

Iboka was a man of Kang'ondu clan. He was not born like
other men. His mother was married but she could not bear
children. Her husband went to the *mugaa* who said: 'To-night
when in the pitch of darkness your wife shall hear the falling
rain let her listen carefully: there will be a child coming out of
heaven, and at dawn it will cry; when it reaches the earth she
must go out and fetch it, and having done so, she must re-enter
with him into the house; she may go and suckle him.' Now
that woman prayed for the rain to rain and, while it was
raining, she heard a baby crying. She went out to fetch him,
and, having fetched him, she returned into the house and
she began to suckle him. At that time the child had two sprout-
ing horns and they were hollowed, but there was no one who
could know what was inside. When the boy grew up, the
mugaa told him: ' Now you have to look after the affairs of the
Tharaka people, because those from the mountains (*rogoro*) destroy them! It happened, then, that robbers, *maitha*, came to
destroy, but when Iboka heard of that, it was then that he performed a great miracle. This is the miracle: he took his two horns
and he put them into two warriors who were brave (*njamba* =
heroes), in this way: he made them sleep, he slit them open
into two parts; then he took one part from one warrior and he
put it together with another part of the other man; he took one
horn and he put it inside and the two parts became one. The
man who was thus produced became a living man (The same
he did with the other parts). It was then that the Tharaka
were very happy, there was no fighting among them, and in
fighting the others those who were killed arose and pursued
their killers destroying many of them. There came a great
famine among the Tharaka and it was impossible to find food.
Some people wishing to eat beans, *nchiabe*, went to the enemies:

MYTHOLOGICAL ORIGINS OF THE UGWE 65

' Do you know? '—' No, we do not know. And what is that you know? '—' There are two warriors among the Tharaka with two horns in their stomach, and with those horns the Tharaka cannot be killed, and even you cannot kill them as you could before.' So those people knew that, perhaps, the people of Tharaka had wisdom. And those who had been looking for food, having received it, returned home. While they were on their way, the enemies came out and followed them till they arrived; and the enemies found a hiding place near the houses. When the night fell, they came out and started fighting. They killed many because they wanted to find out those two young men with the horns in their stomach. Finally they found them alone, killed them, and took the horns. Having taken them they fled. When Iboka heard of this, he became very angry and went out that very night. He travelled for three days, and a fourth and then he entered the rapids called Kiboka. And when he entered there, they tried to follow him but they could not. Iboka entered there, but nobody knows whether he died. There were bananas around there, but now they have become bad; there were trees, but no one can cut them; there were bee-hives, but no one is allowed to collect honey from inside them.

Even today, Kiboka rapids are shown where the Kathita river joins the Thagana. To cut trees at that place is forbidden. If trees are cut, and the offence is not expiated by killing a lamb, the rain will fail.[1]

Another version of the same story introduces the Mugwe in the rôle of Iboka. It was at Tigania that the Tharaka went for food and sold their secret: ' We have come from Tharaka. There is a man there, called Mugwe, who has given us a horn so that we may not be killed. But he is not good.' When they came home, Mugwe left them and

---

[1] Sacred groves of forests wherein no one is, or was, allowed to cut trees are quite common. There are many stories relating to these groves, old and recent, that afford an interesting field of folklore research. See Appendix No. 14.

66 THE MUGWE, A FAILING PROPHET

went away. He left them but they do not know exactly where he went. He disappeared but left his two sons behind: Iboka and Mukumbotha.

This last version shows how the Mugwe has almost entirely ousted Iboka. The function of the Mugwe as the foremost cultural hero of the Meru is even better indicated by the following statements I recorded from an Imenti elder:

Ntangi was the age-class that came with the Mugwe, and this is the one which started to hang up the hives[1]. The next age-class was Rima and they were the first ones to cultivate. Now, with regard to honey being collected, it was this man, called Mugwe, who was first shown that it (the honey) was a help for all men, especially for those who did not have strength, if only they ate the honey like all the others. When he first spoke of the bees, they were not kept in the hives and people did not believe him, but when they saw, they understood that what this man was doing was good. And from that day they understood that the Mugwe was for their good and tried to make them of one idea (*kubagwatithania*). And for this reason they elected him as their father.

Of the age-classes mentioned in the above statements, Ntangi is the first one heading the age-class list of the Imenti, it is one of the four said to have been formed before the Meru migrated from Mbwa. In this way, the function of the Mugwe is related to the very beginning of the Meru, even earlier than the exodus narration has shown. Rima, a term deriving from the verb *ku-rima*, to cultivate, is not mentioned as an age-class in the list of the Imenti, but it is significant that it should be mentioned in relation to the Mugwe in his rôle as the cultural hero of the Meru. As the Mugwe is exalted as the originator of such an important practice as collecting the honey, it must have

---

[1] The Meru hang up beehives in trees.

MYTHOLOGICAL ORIGINS OF THE UGWE 67

seemed only natural that he should also be related to the beginning of such a fundamental agricultural activity as cultivation.

The close relationship of the Mugwe to honey, described in such detail by the cited statements, is a typical feature of the mentality of the Meru, especially the Imenti and the Tharaka. Honey is not only one of the staple elements of the Tharaka diet, it is also, as we shall see, one of the insignia of the Mugwe. Another point that is emphasized by the above statements is the position of the Mugwe in relation to the age-classes. In fact it is the age-classes that are taught by the Mugwe the uses of honey, the way to collect it, and the method for cultivating the soil. It is the age-classes that realize the good influence of the Mugwe in their midst, and it is the age-classes that, having realized this good influence, elect the Mugwe as their father. So the very special relationship of the Mugwe to the age-classes, still found today, has its origin in the very beginnings of the Meru.

4. THE FIRST MUGWE

Up to now we have heard narrations and statements in which the Mugwe has been mentioned generally, i.e. not by his personal name but by his official title. There are other stories in which the personal name is given, a name that actually appears in the lists of the Agwe recorded among the various sub-tribes. When such stories are told, the Mugwe is always described as the first Mugwe, i.e. the one who founded and established the power of the Ugwe. Such a statement is not always consistent with the actual position of the Mugwe mentioned in the list of the Agwe, but must be accepted for the sake of the analysis. Indeed, this is another aspect of the mythopoetical process that goes on with regard to the Mugwe. The first

68 THE MUGWE, A FAILING PROPHET

Mugwe is, thus, another of the cultural heroes, but with more clearly individualized traits.

The first Mugwe of the Igembe was Iguru. Of him it is said that ' he was the first to enter the country of the Igembe '. He it was who set the country free from the waters. The Igembe country in those days, it is said

Was covered with water as if it were a sea, and all the people of Ancene suffered because of it. There was a very great tree, *mukuu*, and this was the reason why the water had been obstructed and remained still. It was Iguru who cut that tree and all the water went down, and all the sufferings of the people came to an end.

Among the Tharaka I recorded the following story about Kirura, the man ' who started the Ugwe '. In the series of the Agwe of the Tharaka he figures in the third place. This is the story:

There was an old man, called Kirura, who had an initiated son, *muthaka*. This man told his son: ' I shall show you the medicines of the Ugwe,' and his son was very pleased. First, however, the father asked his son to help him to enter the great calabash, *gikuru*. The son did what his father had told him and put the old man inside the calabash. Then the father did the same thing with his son: the father was put twice inside the calabash, and the son was put twice. And then the father helped the son a third time, and the son helped the father a third time. It was at this third time that the son ran away. He left his father in the calabash and went away with all the medicines; he left the father, like that, in the calabash. The father, who had been left alone, was taken out by other people of his clan. But, because the father knew all the secrets, he prepared other medicines; he washed his pots and prepared other medicines as those of before. That son went to Ukamba, and there is no one of his house that comes again this way. And the old man had another son who went to Mbere: even

MYTHOLOGICAL ORIGINS OF THE UGWE 69

this one did not want to take his father out of the calabash. Now the father saw that he was left without sons because they had hated him, and he cursed them both. ' Go for ever; you know that you did not take me out of the calabash and that I had to be helped out by other people.' And they went, and, having gone, they divided all the medicines: one went with a certain amount, and the other went with another amount. One went to Mbere, and one went to Ukamba. The medicines of the man of Mbere are more powerful and he can change animals and goats into stones.

The above story is typical of the popular mentality by which everything of wonder far away, is explained in terms of something nearby and accepted as known. So, because the Mbere and the Kamba were famous for their medicines, it was assumed by the Meru elders that those medicines had been stolen by mischievous treachery from their own Mugwe. This story might have been the reason for the opinion formed by some Tharaka elders that there was also a Mugwe among the Kamba and the Mbere: an opinion that did not hold good when I extended my research to those tribes.

5. THE IDENTIFICATION OF THE AGWE WITH THE FIRST MUGWE

Another aspect of the mythological side of the Mugwe is the process of identification between the individual Agwe and the first Mugwe. The phenomenon has already been made evident by the conflicting position of some names in the lists of the Agwe and the statements which describe these names as those of the beginners of the Ugwe. We have mentioned the case of Kirura among the Tharaka. I may here add that the very same elder who dictated the story of Kirura, at another interview, mentioned Gicuthi, ' the man with the tail ', as the originator of the

70 THE MUGWE, A FAILING PROPHET

Ugwe and the first Mugwe. When I pointed out to him the discrepancy with his previous story he did not want to see my point, and stressed that Gicuthe was the first Mugwe and Kirura was also the Mugwe.

The same thing happened whenever I tried to obtain a more definite account of the deeds of past Agwe. It was not always very easy for my informants to distinguish between one Mugwe and another. It was only from the elders of the Mugwe's family, or from those very close to him, that I was able to obtain the series of the Agwe's names. The main reason for the phenomenon may first be found in the nature of the term Mugwe which is an official name. The names in the series are of individuals. But, ' the power of the Mugwe ', as suggested by one of the stories above, is quite distinct from the individual who carries the office. All the holders of the office have been vested in their time with the same power, authority and official name. There can be no difference between them: therefore they may be, and are, in fact, identified.

The case of Mutuampea of the Tharaka illustrates this. Mutuampea was a very great Mugwe, the last of all the Tharaka Agwe to possess the power of the Ugwe in its fullest sense. Then, *Comba* came (' the Europeans and all that '), and the situation in the country was greatly changed. When Mutuampea died, he was succeeded by his son, and then by the present Mugwe, M. Ruanda. The last two were not as great or as successful, as Mutuampea. Therefore Mutuampea has remained in the mind of the Tharaka as the only truly great Mugwe, and his name is mentioned with awe. Mutuampea was the one who led the Tharaka from Mbwa, who divided the land among the clans, who dictated the law, who formed the first age-classes, etc. At the initial stage of my field work

MYTHOLOGICAL ORIGINS OF THE UGWE 71

it was difficult to disentangle the confusing statements, and it was only after some time that I found out that Mutuampea was a man of the past. My first informant, M. Ngoci wa M. Muga of Chokarige, spoke with great fervour and conviction of Mutuampea as the only true leader of the Tharaka. M. Ruanda (the present living Mugwe) was also referred to by the elders equally as ' the Mugwe' or as ' Mutuampea,' so that I could not help forming the idea that Mutuampea was the living Mugwe and the same person as M. Ruanda. It was only when I went to visit M. Ruanda, and pressed my investigation into the genealogy of the Tharaka Agwe that Mutuampea receded to his own past, and the phenomenon became clear. But at that stage I had even been shown the direction of the place where Mutuampea had been buried.

The Meru say that ' the house of the Mugwe cannot come to an end,' (lit. ' always grows ') *mucii jwa Mugwe iukuraga,* or that the Mugwe cannot die. This means that there must be genealogical continuity in the office of the Mugwe. All the Agwe are taken into office because of their genealogical descent from the first Mugwe. The genealogical factor cannot always be substantiated, but it is assumed for certain. The requirement also holds good at present for, as we shall see, a man ' is born to be Mugwe,' i.e. he is primarily elected because of his birth. Another assumption, which we shall consider below, is the descent of all the Agwe of the Meru sub-tribes from one single family. The genealogical factor is also responsible for the identification process that we have noted, by which the deeds of any one of the Agwe can be described as the deeds of the first Mugwe. To each and every one of the Agwe the following statement can be applied: ' *It is for all his good deeds to his people that the Mugwe is acknowledged as Mugwe!* '

72 THE MUGWE, A FAILING PROPHET

6. SOME BELIEFS AND SAYINGS ABOUT THE MUGWE

(*a*) Among the cultural heroes, the men of wonder—*antu ba kurigaria*, who were not born into this world like all the other men, the Tharaka elders of Gatue also mentioned the Mugwe because *he was born with a tail like an animal.* I was later to find out that not only was this strange belief with regard to the Mugwe widespread among the Tharaka, but that it is still applied to the living Mugwe by some of the elders: a further instance of the identification process between the Agwe and the first Mugwe.

It was among the Tharaka of Gatue, in the area around Gatunga market in North Tharaka, that I first recorded this belief; I then recorded it at Rugucha on the border between the Tharaka and the Chuka in South Tharaka; finally I also found it among the Thagichu beyond the Tana River. It is in connection with this belief that the name of the first Mugwe is sometimes recalled as *Gicuthi, Tail* or ' the man with a tail '. Evidently the presence of the tail in the body of the Mugwe is a cause of great wonder and awe. But the tail is also considered the seat and the local source of his power, because on account of it he is not like other men: *nandi gitiru giki ni kio kiari na unene,* ' now it is this tail that has got the power '. And also: *mutiru juu ni ju jumwejaga inya kuthithia mantu jawe,* ' it is this tail that gives him the force (power) by which he can do all his deeds '.

When the elders of Gatue noticed me frowning in bewilderment they appealed, not without some resentment, to the authority of their elders:

Not everybody can see this wonderful thing with his own eyes; not a young initiated man (*muthaka*), not even all the elders. Only the elders of repute, who go to visit the Mugwe twice or thrice in the year, have seen it. These elders who have seen the Mugwe, it is they who come back and tell all these

MYTHOLOGICAL ORIGINS OF THE UGWE 73

things to the others. In Gatue only a hundred elders have seen the Mugwe.

My informants were certain that what they had been told was true. It is relevant to note that all the areas where I recorded this belief are marginal and relatively far from the residence of the Mugwe. For many people living in these areas, the Mugwe has been, and still is, a rather vague figure, a legendary and awe-inspiring man, difficult to approach, who sways all the Tharaka by his authority. But when I went to Chokarige, in the area where the Mugwe lives and is known to everybody as an ordinary man, my enquiries on this belief were answered either with a tolerant and friendly smile or with the blunt retort: ' Is he an animal to have a tail? ' M. Kamunde, the wise old medicine man, said simply: ' I think that all his power comes from God.'

(*b*) In some parts of Meru, I recorded a saying describing the course of the sun by reference to Mukuna-Raku and the Mugwe, a saying still heard, though rarely, today. It is *riua riumagea kwa Mukuna-Ruku, rikathua kwa Mugwe,* ' the sun rises at the place of Mukuna-Ruku and sets at the place of the Mugwe '. Mukuna-Ruku is a name that the Meru apply to a legendary ivory-trader, probably an Arab. The name Mukuna-Ruku means ' beater of the log ' and would refer to the custom of this man to give signals by means of a gong. The connection between Mukuna-Ruku and the sun in this saying could be taken to be simply geographical. The residence of Mukuna-Ruku is said to have been Mombasa, i.e. the east, where the sun rises. But Mukuna-Ruku is also a mythological figure with a body that is all eyes and gives light to the sun. It is therefore from Mukuna-Ruku that the sun draws its powerful forces of light and heat in the morning before he sends

74 THE MUGWE, A FAILING PROPHET

it out on its daily journey.[1] It is more difficult to give a mere geographical interpretation to this saying with regard to the Mugwe, because the geographical connection of the Mugwe with the west cannot so easily be implied. The mythological interpretation affords a better explanation. As we noted above, the house of the Mugwe cannot come to an end, the Mugwe cannot die. It is therefore at his dwelling that the sun sets. The sun, as the Mugwe, cannot fail to give its light and warmth, it cannot die, and therefore it sets at the dwelling of the Mugwe in order to renew its power for the next day. There is a parallel between the two figures of Mukuna-Ruku and the Mugwe, both possessing a very special character and a very special power: light and immortality.

(c) Among the Imenti an unusual aspect of the people's conception of the Mugwe concerns his left hand. It is this hand, as we shall see, that should always hold *kiragu* and be used only to bless. It is a most sacred member of the Mugwe's body and no one is allowed to see it. During the day, the Mugwe spends his time playing *kiothi*, the Meru draughts, but even while he plays, he must always keep his left hand covered and no one must see it. Sudden death would overtake anyone who dared to look at the left hand of the Mugwe.

The above few instances of strange beliefs with regard to the Mugwe may be sufficient to show how his mythological character is deeply rooted in the mentality of the people as a whole. He is indeed a man of wonder, a man who is not born like other, common men.

---

[1] G. St. J. Orde Brown, 1925, p. 217, writes as follows: ' the Mwimbe say that the sun is sent out from the house of Mukuna-Ruku, whose body is all eyes. There are many bridges to his house far away in the East.'

MYTHOLOGICAL ORIGINS OF THE UGWE 75

7. THE UGWE AND THE MERU

The foregoing analysis of the mythological origins of the Mugwe throws light on a most interesting aspect of the attitude of the Meru towards the Mugwe. The position of the Mugwe in the old Meru social structure was paramount: he was the chief, the leader, the protector of the people. There seems to be no corresponding paramount position in the early mythological narrations of the past history of the Meru. Other heroes and other leaders, such as Komenjue, were the central figures of these legends. It was natural for the elders, who greatly respected the Mugwe, to feel the urge to try and redress the mythological balance. Hence the obvious efforts to build up the position of the Mugwe and to force him into the unique rôle of the all-chief, all-father, all-saviour, gradually obscuring all other leaders and heroes. The mythological exaltation of the Mugwe thus explains and justifies his paramount authority in the structure of the Meru and gives it a basis and foundation in their early history. The vitality of the cultural heroes other than the Mugwe shows that this mythopoetical phenomenon was still in process. It shows also that the institution of Mugwe is a relatively recent one, though it does not imply that it is not indigenous to the Meru. Indeed, the mythological process has had a further important result, by which a sort of identification between the Ugwe and ' Meru-ness,' between the Mugwe and the Meru, has been established. In the words of the elders: *unene bwawe (bwa Mugwe) bwaumire na aria Ameru baumire,* ' his (of the Mugwe) power came out, originated, from where the Meru came out, or took their origin '; and also: *ni we munene wetu kuuma kenya,* ' it is he our chief *from the beginning* '. The implication of these sentences, and many other similar ones, is merely that the Ugwe is not a power imported to the Meru from outside,

THE MUGWE, A FAILING PROPHET

but an indigenous power of their own stock, of the same origin, and the same beginning. The Meru ' came out ' from Mbwa; it was at this ' crossing ' point that they reached a consciousness of their unity as a people, a consciousness that was not extinguished by their later divisions into sub-tribes. At this very same point the Ugwe was also found, and the Mugwe was, at least mythologically, the leader of all the Meru. It follows that to be genuinely a Meru, one must live under the Mugwe. All this seems to contrast with the sectional divisions of the Meru that are described as alien to the Mugwe (Urio of the Tharaka, Athwana of the Tigania). We must note, however, how these sectional divisions are overcome in practice by their acceptance of the Mugwe's authority. They, in any case, become irrelevant in the minds of the elders who tend to extend, in a mythological fashion, the power of the Mugwe to all that is Meru. It is, indeed, by an expression of this mythological origin or process that the Mugwe, as was reported at the beginning of this study, may sometimes be called ' the king ' of the Meru.

Chapter Four

'BORN TO BE MUGWE'
(*Mugwe we ni guciarwa*)

The power of the Mugwe is not obtainable by conquest, nor is it a profession open to anyone with skill or vocation. It is an hereditary power, which has been handed down from father to son within the same family for generations. Genealogical descent is therefore the primary qualification for a candidate to the power of the Ugwe, hence the saying *Mugwe we ni guciarwa*, ' one is born to be Mugwe '. We shall see, however, that, once the hereditary principle is assured, the choice of the candidate is also determined by other considerations and factors regarding his moral character.

Among the Igembe we noticed how the hereditary nature of the Mugwe proper distinguishes him from the Mugwe-diviner. Indeed, the hereditary principle is a basic requirement of the Ugwe among all the sub-tribes. It obtains also with the assistant Agwe of the Chuka and with the Mukiama of the Athwana Tigania.

I. THE ORIGINAL FAMILY UNITY OF THE AGWE

The hereditary principle is supported by myths which assert that all the Agwe are descended from the same family. This assertion provides another piece of evidence with regard to the mythological origins of the Ugwe in general. Moreover, the genealogical unity of the Agwe throughout Meru is constantly assumed and sometimes strongly asserted.

78 THE MUGWE, A FAILING PROPHET

When I was in Tharaka, I remember speaking with an elder of Kiramana age-class, called Rocaoru. He appeared to be versed in the lore of the Ugwe, and spoke very fully of the virtues proper to the Mugwe. When I asked him whether all that he was telling me of the Tharaka Mugwe could also be applied to the Mugwe of the other Meru sub-tribes, this was his answer: *batiri mwanya, ni untu ni ba muntu umwe, ni ba ithe umwe*, ' they are not different, because they are of the same man, they are of the same father '. I heard similar statements later on, among all the Meru. M. Kiganka, the Mugwe of the Chuka, once told me: ' everywhere there are the Agwe, and this is the reason that the Tharaka, the Igembe, the Chuka, and also the others, are children of the same man ', *ni nthaka cia muntu umwe*. Among the Imenti I recorded the following: ' all the Agwe acknowledge each other, even if they live far apart, because they are of the same extraction: the Chuka, the Tharaka, the Igembe, the Tigania and the Imenti '.

The Tharaka state also that the clan of the Agwe is the same everywhere, though names are different. Of all the Agwe the Tharaka say *ni ba Kithuri*, ' they are of Kithuri ', because Kithuri is the clan of their Mugwe. When I pointed out to the elders that among the other Meru sub-tribes the clan of the Mugwe was not in fact *Kithuri*, they simply remarked, ' what *Kithuri* is among the Tharaka, *Umu* is for the Imenti, and so on '.

The stories that embody the tradition of the original unity of the Agwe can be classified into two groups; one claiming Chuka as the starting place of the Agwe's diffusion among the Meru sub-tribes; and another claiming Tharaka. The latter is the more common. The Chuka stories refer particularly to the relationship of the Mugwe of Chuka with the Mugwe of Igembe. One

'BORN TO BE MUGWE'

version, dictated by a group of elders from Chuka, runs as follows:

Once upon a time there was an old man called Mukunga. The old man had two children, a boy and a girl. It came to pass that the boy had intercourse with his sister and she conceived and bore a son. This is the man called Karieni, and he became the Mugwe of Igembe. His father was the Mugwe of Chuka.

While, among the Chuka, I found that the relationship of their Mugwe with the Mugwe of the Igembe was a general tradition, i.e. known to a very great number of elders, among the Igembe I did not discover any counterpart or any special reference to a similar relationship, though I did not fail to make enquiries on this point.

The Tharaka tradition is more widespread among the Meru sub-tribes. Its *leit-motif* is the Mugwe from Tharaka bringing relief in time of distress to the other sub-tribes and settling among his guests. One early version has it that the Mugwe of the Tharaka went to assist the Igembe, who were in trouble: while he was there he established the Ugwe among them. But while the Mugwe was away, the Tharaka were also struck by famine and their suffering became great. So the elders of the Tharaka went to Igembe to recall their Mugwe. The latter did not want to leave the Igembe, but he did not entirely refuse the elders from Tharaka. He sent his son back to Tharaka, giving him some of his sacred things that were necessary for the Ugwe, though he did not give him everything. M. Ruanda, the present Mugwe of the Tharaka, who was present while I recorded the above story, commented with a typical expression of mythological identification: ' This is the reason that you do not see me with many things now! '

80 THE MUGWE, A FAILING PROPHET

Another version holds that it was the son of the Tharaka Mugwe who went among the Igembe to start the Ugwe.

A modified version of the same story is also found among the Igembe. The Mugwe of the Tharaka went among the Igembe at a time of famine when they were suffering greatly. He established the Ugwe among them, and by that the Igembe were relieved of their trouble. After that, however, the old man, being an old man, felt homesick and returned to his home among the Tharaka: 'It is always hard,' commented the Igembe elders, 'for an old man to leave the place of his fathers.' On returning he left his son who became the Mugwe of the Igembe.

Also the Mugwe of the Imenti is said by the Tharaka elders to have come from among the Tharaka. It was again during a period of distress and suffering that the Mugwe from Tharaka went to Imenti to relieve them. He helped them until their troubles came to an end and as a reward was offered a girl as a wife. He then decided to settle among the Imenti. It is for this reason, it is also said, that the Tharaka of Urio could go and visit the Mugwe of the Imenti at Kirirwa.

I did not record any special version of the above stories among the Tigania, but the statement of the old Mugwe, M. Ikwenga, that the Tigania did not have their Mugwe when they came from Mbwa, but 'we selected him afterwards, because our children were becoming very sick', seems to support the Tharaka tradition.

Another version of the Tharaka tradition, as told by some of their elders, is somehow connected with the story of Iboka. The Mugwe, like Iboka, became displeased with the Tharaka. He left them and disappeared, nobody knew where. However, he left a small son who eventually married a Tharaka girl. She bore him a large number of

1a. M. Ruanda, the Mugwe of the Tharaka, blessing his people. Behind him is one of his assistant elders. See page 110.

1b. A group of Imenti youngsters dressed for a circumcision festival.

2a. M. Kiganka, the Mugwe of the Chuka. See page 43.

2b. M. Muga (right), the blind elder of Chokarige, and Nkeya, the old circumciser of the Tharaka. See page 153.

'BORN TO BE MUGWE' 81

sons, and they all became Agwe, the forefathers of the present ones.

All these traditions might be taken as evidence of a common family origin for all the Agwe, and of the Tharaka being the first among the Meru to possess the Ugwe. As it happens, however, they are vague and even contradictory, and cannot be substantiated by actual evidence. The important point to be noted here is that the original unity of the Agwe is taken for granted to justify some present situations or to stress the mutual relations of the Agwe. In this way, the above traditions acquire a real structural significance. We have noted the case of M. Ruanda who, in all seriousness, attributed his present poverty to the emigration of his forefathers to Igembe. A most striking instance of the same attitude was provided by the Mugwe of the Chuka, M. Kiganka. Acting on the assumption that the Mugwe of the Igembe was specially related to the Mugwe of the Chuka, as is told by the above Chuka tradition, M. Kiganka sought relief in his present tragic situation from the Mugwe of the Igembe. I had to act as an intermediary between the two Agwe, as I shall describe later on. Though, for various reasons, the transaction came to nothing, it showed clearly the practical significance and consequences of the mythological foundations of the Ugwe.

A further point to be noted is the relatively recent appearance of the Mugwe as described in the above stories. The Mugwe is not there from the very beginning but he arrives, or is called, at a time of distress when the settlement of the sub-tribe has already occurred. This recent appearance seems to contradict the narrations and the statements that the Mugwe has always been with the Meru since they came out of Mbwa. On the other hand, our previous deduction seems to indicate that the

82 THE MUGWE, A FAILING PROPHET

high position of the Mugwe, by which he is identified with his own sub-tribe, is due to a clear mythopoetical process. By this process the Mugwe is made to replace all previous heroes of the Meru sub-tribes, he is described as performing wonders and great deeds and so he is introduced as the leader and chief of all that is Meru.

2. THE HEREDITARY PRINCIPLE AND THE RIGHT OF PRIMOGENITURE

While the Ugwe is considered as the patrimony of a family, *mucii*, or of its lineage, *mwiriga*, it is not a power that can be inherited collectively by all the members of that lineage. Only one is the heir, and only one can be elected to take over the family's heritage by becoming the Mugwe. It is, therefore, in the nature of the Ugwe, as a form of authority, that it should be an individual power. It follows that there is a real distinction between the Mugwe and the other ' lay ' members of his clan, in the same way as there is a distinction, more or less rational, between the Mugwe as an individual and the power of the Ugwe that he holds. The individual character of the Ugwe was expressed by M. Kiganka, the Mugwe of the Chuka in one of his vigorous statements: *oni ndaciarirwe na bu. Kinya tugaciaragwa na antu ikumi omwe ni we athuragwa*, 'I have been born with that [the power of the Ugwe]. Even if ten of us are born, only one is consecrated.'

As a consequence of the hereditary succession, one would expect that the choice of the candidate to the Ugwe would consistently fall on the first-born son of the Mugwe. This is not always the case. It is clearly stated by the elders that other considerations, apart from the genealogical one, must be kept in mind at the time of the choice of a new Mugwe. The person of the Mugwe is sacred and his office is a very high one, therefore no unworthy character, though he be the first-born son of the Mugwe, may assume such profound and holy dignity. A candidate must be ' as good of heart as his father ', *ari na nkoro njega ta ithe*. If the first-born son of the Mugwe is not eligible, the choice for the next Mugwe may fall on another member of the Mugwe's lineage and family, but he must have a good character, mental alertness and fitness, legal and moral probity. All these requirements are, no doubt, of a very high standard and we shall analyse them when we speak of the virtues proper to the Mugwe.

Some genealogical evidence will make the issue of the primogeniture clearer. (Capital letters indicate the names of the Agwe; the initial W. stands for wife.)

The Mugwe of Chuka. Clan: *Nkui*.

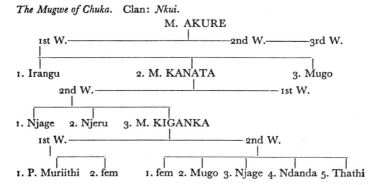

M. Akure, the great-grandfather of M. Kiganka, was the Mugwe. His first-born son, Irangu, did not succeed him. The choice fell on M. Kanata, the second-born son. M. Kanata had no male issue from his first wife; among the sons of his other wife the choice favoured M. Kiganka, the youngest of his three sons, who is the present Mugwe. M. Kiganka's first-born son, Pankratio Muriithi, was killed by the Mau Mau, but it was very unlikely that he would have been chosen because he was a baptized Christian. At present, M. Kiganka has not made up his mind, but he seems to regard the very young Thathi as the most suitable candidate. Thus, among the Chuka, for the last two generations no Mugwe has been the first-born son of his father.

The Mugwe of Igembe. Clan: *Ncenge.*

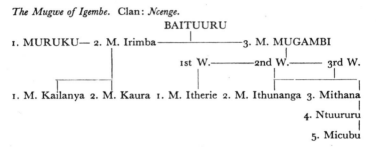

Baituuru was succeeded by his eldest son, Muruku, who is still alive. He stayed in office for two successive age-classes. M. Mugambi was chosen as the next Mugwe in preference to his older brother, M. Irimba. M. Itherie, the first-born son of M. Mugambi, seems to have been brought up with the idea that he should become the next Mugwe. He has chosen, however, to be a school teacher, and as he wants to become a Christian his election as the next Mugwe seems now to be out of the question. No one, I found, was willing to commit himself to naming a probable candidate to succeed M. Itherie. One point is worth noting, namely, that while the succession of the Agwe among the Igembe is more closely related to the formation of the age-classes than among the other tribes, this does not seem to affect in any special way the hereditary principle of succession. M. Mugambi, though he did not want to commit himself, said that most probably either M. Kailanya or M. Kaura would be selected as the next Mugwe.

The Mugwe of Tharaka. Clan: *Kithuri.*

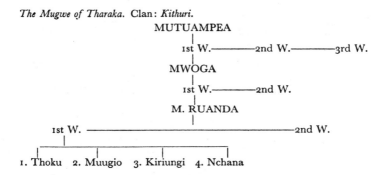

The succession among the Tharaka during the past two generations has been in favour of the first-born son.

Of the above three genealogical cases examined, it is only in the last one of the Tharaka that the right of the first-born is observed. In the other cases, the observance is not consistent. Probably, however, the choice of a candidate, other than the first-born son, does not in itself constitute absolute evidence that the right of primogeniture is not a firm principle in the succession to the office of the Mugwe. In fact it could still be argued that a newly elected Mugwe, on taking over the paramountcy of the office, accedes also to the rôle of the first-born, because by right of office he becomes the most senior member of his lineage and family, as if he were considered by a *fictio juris* to be the true first-born son. The argument is consistent with the position of the Mugwe in the social structure of the Meru, and is supported by the description of the prerogatives and status of the Mugwe.

86 THE MUGWE, A FAILING PROPHET

3. THE TRAINING OF A CANDIDATE FOR THE OFFICE OF MUGWE

A long time before a Mugwe is formerly elected or takes over, he must be nominated as a candidate in order that he may be properly trained for his high station in life. As has been said, the nomination must fall on a member of the Mugwe's lineage. The candidate's nomination is not a formal thing, but the decision is a privilege of the Mugwe, who is assisted by his family's elders and by the elders of his age-class.

Among the Chuka, it is the Mugwe who indicates which of his sons will be his successor, ' in the same way,' commented M. Kiganka, ' as a king says which of his sons is to succeed him as a new king.' The nomination, among the Imenti, is also done by the Mugwe. If the candidate is to be the Mugwe's brother's son, the candidate's father will be officially informed. Two elders are chosen by the Mugwe and sent to the genitor of the boy. The errand is officially known as *mureegi 'o Mugwe* (*wa Mugwe*), ' the errand of the Mugwe '. The genitor will be informed that the Mugwe has set his eyes on his son and that he has nominated him to be the candidate for succession to the office of the Mugwe; the genitor, therefore, will have to take greater care in the education of his son. He will see that he is protected from anything or any work that might endanger the bodily perfection that is one of the primary requirements of the candidate to the power of the Ugwe. The candidate's body must not suffer any cut or blow, and therefore the candidate is not supposed to cut wood or fetch water for anyone. For this reason he will not be allowed to share the life of the other youngsters in the *gaaru*, for there the young initiate might be forced to suffer base trials and bodily pains, such as beatings and menial labours, inflicted by his seniors. An even higher degree of

'BORN TO BE MUGWE' 87

purity will be required from the candidate in his moral behaviour. It is the responsibility of the genitor, of the Mugwe, and of the elders (who were his sponsors to the genitor at the time of the ' errand of the Mugwe ') to look after the candidate's moral education by warnings and special instructions. He will thus follow very closely the activities of the elders in their official assemblies, in order that he may learn their ways and the lore of his people. Apart from his sacred character, his training, at this stage, is not very different from the training of a *mugambi*. His early sharing of the life of the elders deprives the candidate of the normal development in education followed by all the other youngsters. But their standards must not be his standards, his office is far too high. He must conform to the best, almost to an idealized standard of life, for this is the necessary background to his being the future leader, protector and father of his people. (See *The moral virtues of the Mugwe*, p. 105.)

The above method and ideals of training were applied not only among the Imenti but among all the other Meru sub-tribes. Among the Chuka I was told also that special stress was laid on the professional side of the candidate's training. He was given a small bag, *kiondo*, of a similar type to the one used by the Mugwe, containing ' things ' similar to the sacred ones used by the Mugwe. A special elder was also appointed by the Mugwe to look after him, and both the sponsor and the Mugwe assisted him throughout his training, until, finally, they would sponsor him as the new Mugwe to the council of the elders.

The Igembe elders stated that the nomination of a candidate could still occur at a time when he was an uninitiated boy, *mwiji*; but, in that case, he would very soon be initiated and introduced to the way of life of the elders.

88 THE MUGWE, A FAILING PROPHET

4. THE DEATH OF THE MUGWE AND THE ACCESSION OF HIS SUCCESSOR

There are at least two ways in which a new Mugwe takes office, now and in the recent past. One is followed by the Chuka, the Tharaka, and the Imenti, the other by the Tigania and the Igembe. The first system is distinguished by the Mugwe's lifelong tenure of the office, the latter by the coincidence of the Mugwe's term of office with the ruling period of an age-class. In the first system, the term of office lasts for life and is terminated at the old Mugwe's death. In the words of M. Kiganka: *Baaba kagita karia agakua ni rio mwana agakarira giti kiu*, ' at the time of my father's death, his son [M. Kiganka himself] was made to sit on this stool '. The two systems are also distinguished by the degree of importance attached to the death of the Mugwe by the two groups of sub-tribes. Among the Chuka, the Tharaka, and the Imenti the death of the Mugwe is an event of public mourning. Among the Tigania and the Igembe it remains a private family concern that may pass almost unnoticed outside. The reason is to be found in the early retirement of the Mugwe, after which his status is no longer that of a Mugwe proper, but of an ordinary respected elder. It is, therefore, only with the first group that the death of the Mugwe takes on any special significance.

The elders of the Mugwe's lineage are expected to be present at his passing from this life, and are summoned to listen to his last requests. The dying Mugwe will first be asked what name he wishes to give to the next ruling age-class. He will then call out his son, whom he has nominated to be his successor, and, in the presence of the elders, will remind him of the greatness of his office, recalling all his previous instructions.

When the Mugwe's death is publicly known, people

'BORN TO BE MUGWE' 89

from all over the country assemble for mourning. The Mugwe is always buried. Among the Meru, as well as the Kikuyu, burial was not customary except for very rich and famous elders. The sons of the dead man have to perform the ceremony while the elders of the clan assemble for the rites that follow a man's death and accompany his burial. The assistance of the *mwinji*, the ritual cleaner (lit. ' barber '), is always sought in such circumstances. But with the Mugwe the *mwinji* is not summoned, for he is regarded as impure because of his very profession. It is the wife of the Mugwe who will clean his body, and she also cures the hides of the ram, *nturumi*, and the he-goat, *nthenge*, which have been ritually killed by the elders. The hides are used to cover the body of the Mugwe while it is carried and arranged in the grave. The grave is always situated under the mound of refuse, *kiara*, on the entrance side of the house, a place that was generally regarded with awe for this very reason.

The grave of the Mugwe is not a centre of pilgrimage, nor is it specially honoured except by vague memories. Thus, among the Tharaka, I was struck by the reverence with which the elders would indicate and point out the direction of the grave of Mutuampea. At Kirirwa, among the Imenti, whenever the elders assemble for a meeting of their councils they offer a libation of beer on the entrance side of the house to honour the memory of the Mugwe. A similar practice, however, was more or less general with the elders at their assemblies, its purpose being to honour the ancestors.

The death of the Mugwe was soon followed by the accession and proclamation of the new Mugwe. The occasion was one of extraordinary solemnity for all. In the words of M. Kiganka: *Antu bonthe ba Chuka, na twana, na aka, ni bejaga kuona nkuethua Mugwe. Antu baba bejaga na*

90 THE MUGWE, A FAILING PROPHET

mburi, na irio, na uuki, na nthenge, ni untu bwa Mugwe, 'all
the people of Chuka, the children, the women, came to see
how I was made the Mugwe. All of them came with
goats, food, honey-beer, for the new Mugwe'. The
occasion is really unique, and it is the only time when
women and children are allowed to be present at an
official function of the Mugwe. M. Kiganka noted that at
such festivals there was plenty of honey-beer which
enabled him to bless all his people and let them enjoy it.

Among the Tigania and the Igembe, the accession of a
new Mugwe coincides with the festival of the *ntuiko*. By
this festival a new age-class takes power, which indicates
how closely connected the Mugwe of the Tigania and the
Igembe are with the age-class system. The Mugwe of these
sub-tribes is, personally, a member of the previous class
in the same alternation as the age-class that takes over.
His structural position within the age-class system makes
him the visible link between the old age-classes and the
new one. For the same reason he is regarded as the
father, leader, and protector of the new age-class. He
himself is the synthesis of the status of all the fathers of the
age-class members, and thus he is singled out to be the
father of his people, not unlike the Mugwe of the Chuka
the Tharaka and the Imenti, who, being in office for life,
can better claim to possess such general parental authority
over their people.

The ritual of accession is not performed at the same time.
In fact the time for the *ntuiko* is chosen to suit the requirements of every section, as was noted with the Athwana
and Igoki sections of the Tigania.[1] In spite of these diverg-
encies in time the actual ritual is very similar. It can be
divided into three stages. The first stage is the pro-

---

[1] The Athwana call the *ntuiko, gukora gaaru,* stressing the function of the
gaaru in the initiation of new members.

clamation of the new Mugwe and the sacrifice of the *ntigiri* bull which marks the opening of the *ntuiko*. The matter is first arranged by the elders who sponsor the new age-class and the leaders of the retiring age-class. The news of the proclamation of the new Mugwe is soon spread throughout the country.[1] The sacrifice of the *ntigiri* bull was a very special one. Not all the elders are eligible to take part in it, but only the Mugwe and a number of delegates who must be free from any impurity or sin (*bakumenya bati na weya*, ‘ they know to be without sin ’), and who are not blacksmiths. A sort of a procession is formed, taking the beast into the forest, which can be at the top of Mt. Nyambene or on the plain towards the Imenti country.[2]

The term *ntigiri*, by which the bull is known, means literally ‘ donkey ’. The term so applied to a sacrificial beast sounds odd, but no elder was ever able to offer an explanation. It seems likely that its use derives from a corruption of the word *ntindiri* which became *ntigiri*. This seems more probable if one considers that the donkey was unknown to the Meru, as to all the so called Hamitic-Bantu, until very recently, when they borrowed it from the neighbouring Nilo-Hamites and Hamites. If the original term for the sacrificial bull was *ntindiri*, then the extension of the term, used for aged men and women who are distinguished for their sacred character, becomes significant. The bull for the sacrifice is *ntindiri*, not because of its old age, but because it has been set aside for a sacred use and is therefore holy. The colour of the beast

[1] It was in this way that I came to know of the proclamation of the new Mugwe of the Tigania-Igoki, M. Kirimi, during May 1956.

[2] In 1955 I visited the lower forest, described as *giitho kia Mukiama*, the forest of the Mukiama. It was a grove, not large, crossed by a small water-course, which formed a small pool, covered with water plants and flowers. Being able to see the water under the leaves was a sign that God was pleased with the Mukiama.

92 THE MUGWE, A FAILING PROPHET

must always be black, a colour sacred to God.[1] The skin of the animal must be preserved and cured for the use of the Mugwe. The sacrifice of the *ntigiri* (or *ntindiri*) bull ' sanctifies ', *ibathuriete*, the new age-class and establishes the authority of the new Mugwe.

The second stage of the ritual consists in the actual preparation of the sacred mantle. During this time all members of the new age-class enjoy a privileged and sacred status: they tour the country from house to house and are entitled to enter freely. It is a time when many abuses are silently endured by women and house-owners. In the meantime the new age-class will pay to the retiring age-class and their sponsors their *ntuiko*-fees in the form of a number of goats.

The third stage can be very solemn. The new Mugwe is formally and officially presented with his black mantle, and while he receives the homage of the new age-class he blesses them and all the people with a libation of honey-beer. The Mugwe is also officially entrusted with the other insignia of his office, which we shall describe presently.

The two systems of accession seem to indicate a different position of the Mugwe in his own sub-tribe. There is no doubt that, while among the Tigania and the Igembe the individual Mugwe is associated with the period of an age-class, among the other sub-tribes his position is much more personal. In this latter case the Mugwe's period of office does not coincide with the power of one age-class, but starts independently of any age-class and comes to an end, naturally, as it were, with his death. In both systems, however, the *ntuiko*, the rite of passage from one class to another, remains under the control and blessing of the

---

[1] The idea of the sacred character of black is also peculiar to the Masai. *Engai Narok*, God Black, is the Masai good God who sends the rain in plenty (black clouds).

'BORN TO BE MUGWE' 93

Mugwe. It is the function at which he wears formally all the insignia of his office. In the same way, everything else of general concern comes under the control of the Mugwe, even within the latter group of sub-tribes, so that the relationship between the Mugwe and his people is very deep and intimate.

Indeed, it is typical of the personal position the Mugwe enjoys among the Imenti, Chuka, and Tharaka, that the most positive statements with regard to his authority have been recorded among them. However, notwithstanding this apparent and actual differentiation, the two systems do not show any essential diversity in the position of the Mugwe. In fact, among none of the Meru sub-tribes is there ever a break in the effective continuity of the Ugwe, so that the old Meru saying ' the Mugwe does not die ' holds good for both systems.

In the ritual of accession of the new Mugwe there were some parts that fell to women. Among the Imenti, a wretched old woman was summoned to be the victim in a somewhat strange and brutal ordeal which the newly elected Mugwe was expected to surmount. All the elders of the Mugwe's clan, Omo, assembled at some chosen spot where ' that very old woman ', *mwekuru umwe mukuru muno*, was also to be present. The elected Mugwe was asked to take hold of the woman and to race with her, always keeping hold of her hand, running as fast as possible. If the old woman died in the racing, the elected Mugwe was considered fit to take office and could be proclaimed as the new Mugwe, otherwise the proclamation was postponed. The issue of the race, in any case, was certain beforehand because care was taken to select a really very old woman.[1]

[1] The ritual of the accession of the new Mugwe recorded by Father Ghilardi of the Igoji Catholic Mission, describes the Mugwe as being

94   THE MUGWE, A FAILING PROPHET

The elders always refused, or declared themselves to be unable, to give an explanation of this ordeal. Its significance may lie, I suggest, in the supernatural quality that distinguishes the *ntindiri* men and women, of whom the old woman was one. The Mugwe too must possess this supernatural quality. He must avoid sin, he is considered to be very near to God, not unlike the *ntindiri* elders. As the Mugwe is the chief and leader of all, he must also be higher and above all, even the *ntindiri*. Before his proclamation as the new Mugwe takes place, his holiness is put to the test. If the woman succumbs in the ordeal, it is because the supernatural power of the Mugwe has overwhelmed hers; if she survives, then the candidate is not yet considered fit.

5. THE INSIGNIA OF THE MUGWE

The reference to a stool, *giti*, by M. Kiganka, in the statement quoted above regarding his succession, made me inquisitive as to whether there was any sacred stool handed over to the Mugwe as a symbol of his power. Nothing of the sort existed, the reference being entirely metaphorical. There is, in fact, a small carved stool that the elders are privileged to carry, especially when they assemble in council. Because of this privilege, it is regarded as a symbol of the elder's authority. The word *giti*, stool, may also refer to the rights of a man over a piece of land, or simply to the lands itself, *kithaka*. With reference to the Mugwe, the metaphorical implications of the term are evident. The Mugwe's *giti* is his authority

crowned and put into office by an old woman, *mwekuru umukuru muno*, who after the ceremony was expected to retire and die. The recorder and his informants, who were educated Meru, suggested that poison was very probably administered to make sure that she would die. It was thought that, having touched the Mugwe with her hands, she should no longer be allowed to live.

'BORN TO BE MUGWE'

as the leader and chief of his people; it is also his land, i.e., on account of his being Mugwe, all the land of his people.[1] The elders, who carry a stool, are the heads of their families, and the actual owners of the family's land, and have also a claim on the land of their clans as such: in a similar way, the Mugwe carries a symbolical stool, his power, which makes him the head of such a great family as his people, and the supreme owner of all their land.

The insignia of the Mugwe are a distinction of his office. At the same time they are regarded as the symbols of the country and the people's prosperity. The Mugwe is their custodian and keeper. The skin-mantle, the crown or the hood, the staff, the honey-beer, and the *kiragu*, are the most common insignia. They are evaluated differently in the various sub-tribes, as we shall presently see.

The skin-mantle is first to be considered in its general use. In the past it was the only form of garment worn by the Meru. It is still to be seen nowadays especially in some remote parts of the country. Children and young men used one of a smaller size. The elders wore a larger one, black or dark in colour. The latter was, thus, a feature of the elderhood and a mark of distinction. One of the present-day chiefs, M. Muraa, though he has entirely adopted European dress, frequently wears a dark-coloured skin-mantle, as a small cape over his jacket, explaining that ' the skin-mantle is an old Meru symbol of authority '. The Mugwe wore his mantle when he officially ' blessed ' his people and his country.

The Mugwe's skin-mantle was of the type worn by the elders. It was offered to him at the time of his accession by the members of the age-class he blessed, and it could always be renovated when worn out. All the Mugwe's

---

[1] In modern usage, *mwene giti*, lit. ' the owner of the chair', is the Meru translation for the English ' chairman '.

96   THE MUGWE, A FAILING PROPHET

clothes, in any case, should be presented to him by his people, as he should also be assisted in all his needs: 'if he were to go naked, his nakedness would be a shame over his people ': *utheru bwawe ni bwari na nthoni muno kiri antu.*

The making of the Mugwe's skin-mantle was always an occasion, many prescriptions having to be observed. The skins must be of sheep or goat, though the hide of a sacrificial bull could also be used. The colour must be black or, at least, dark. The skin must not be pierced or pegged for drying. No needle or knife was to be used; it was only to be touched by the hands of men. 'It is a great job to make it,' remarked an elder from Tigania. 'Two groups of men took it in turn to hold the skin until it was dried and properly cured with fat.' In Imenti the rule was that the preparation of the skin-mantle for the Mugwe was not to be suspended during the night, other-wise the *ntuntuguru* and the *ndugweka* birds (large owls) would stir up such a noise as to make it impossible to rest. Now-adays even the Agwe wear blankets; but whenever they make an appearance in their official capacity, they do so by wearing the sacred skin-mantle. At Antubociu, among the Igembe, the skin-mantle has assumed an esoteric character: it is not shown to anyone, except the initiates at official, functions. M. Kiganka of the Chuka lost all his property in the conflagration that destroyed his house. But, under his blanket, he still wore a skin-cloth (a rather old one) which, he stated, he could never be parted from because it was the only symbol of his authority ' that nobody could take away from him ', and the substitute, *ithenyene*, for what he had lost.

Among the Imenti there was a special feast, called *ntumo ya nguo*, ' the sewing of the garment ', celebrated by the Imenti women at the time when the news of the next *ntuiko* was spread. The reason for the event was that the

'BORN TO BE MUGWE' 97

young men, who had been living in the *gaaru,* had completed their training period and were about to be formed
into an age-class. Their life in the *gaaru* was to end for
good. Events of this sort were entirely restricted to men.
Women, officially, should not know anything about it,
but to let them know indirectly so that they ' would not
be afraid of the new age-class (*nthuki*) ', the young brides,
aciere, prepared a skin-mantle and the day for *ntumo ya
nguo* was proclaimed. On that day there was food, drink
and dancing. At a certain time of day, the skin-mantle was
produced and two of the young brides were chosen to race
for it. The skin-mantle was handed to one of the two racers,
while the second was supposed to fight the first for the
mantle. Having won the mantle she would run away and
hide it. But the first girl would run after her and take back
the mantle. The mantle having been thus rescued, the old
women would come forth and take hold of the mantle
' now we have it and we shall keep it '. At the end, the
skin-mantle was handed over to the new elders: ' take ye
this, and keep it until next time (when another age-class
will come forth) '.

From this time on, the young men would no longer live
in the *gaaru.* Though it is certain that the Mugwe was
presented with a skin-mantle by the members of an age-
class, it is not clear whether that mantle presented to the
age-class members by their womenfolk was the one offered
to the Mugwe. It does not seem likely.

The ceremony of handing over the mantle to the
Mugwe was a very solemn one. It coincided with the
ntuiko among the Igembe and Tigania, while among the
Imenti and the Chuka, though it was performed also at
the *ntuiko,* it took place first at the accession of the new
Mugwe. The Mugwe donned the mantle ceremonially
and blessed all those present: ' On that day he could

98 THE MUGWE, A FAILING PROPHET

truly realize that he was a great man.' All the elders and the warriors were assembled together. Everybody else had also to celebrate. To the elders and the warriors, the Mugwe offered two bulls to mark the festivity. Even the sick were asked to attend, and they were eager to do so, ' for they could recover from their disease on that day '.[1]

The mantle of the Mugwe was always cured with ram fat. Among the Igembe, where the skin-mantle is regarded as the highest symbol of the Mugwe's authority, the mantle was destroyed at the time of the election of the new Mugwe and the remains were buried under the refuse mound (*kiara*) at the side of the hut entrance. The Mugwe of the Tharaka does not, at present, wear any mantle. His power is now centred on the custody and use of the sacred honey-beer. But in the past the use of the sacred mantle also seems to have been observed by the Tharaka Mugwe. There are statements by some elders asserting this and it is also said that those of Urio were expected to present the Mugwe with a mantle at the time of the formation of the age-class.

M. Kiganka of Chuka mentioned also a cap, *nkubia*, as among the insignia of the Mugwe. He referred to a monkey-skin hood usually worn by other distinguished elders. M. Ruanda of the Tharaka always made a point of wearing such a hood at our meetings. It does not seem to be used by the Igembe and the Tigania. The Mugwe here has another type of head-dress (*mungi*) worn also by other distinguished elders. It is a special

---

[1] In 1934 Father Comoglio of the Consolata Mission, who had been living at Chera for some months and was (and still is) a personal friend of M. Kiganka, witnessed one of these functions. He describes vividly how the elders and the warriors of the Chuka had crowded together in the large plain of Chera Village, and how they passed in an orderly fashion before M. Kiganka, who in his official attire as their Mugwe, blessed every one of them, to the accompaniment of the high-pitched song: *ni we Mugwe, ni we Mugwe*, ' you are the Mugwe, you are the Mugwe '.

'BORN TO BE MUGWE' 99

strap of goatskin, black in colour, and usually neatly combed and cleaned.

The staff is a more definite distinction of the Mugwe, though its use is also general among the elders. The staff of the Mugwe must be a large straight stick, and its colour is the ritual black. It may be decorated at the tip with ostrich feathers. Some Tigania elders stressed a difference between the common straight staff used by an ordinary elder and a hooked staff described as a distinction of the members of Gaita and Akiuna clans. With this staff the Gaita could perform wonders, such as bringing anything to an end. This belief in the power of the Gaita people is connected with the wonders performed by Gaita at the crossing of the water. Indeed the staff, as part of the insignia of the Mugwe, must be related to the use of the staff by the first Mugwe who did great things with it. Any present Mugwe can do the same. ' When the Igembe people came here to get the Ugwe,' narrated M. Kiganka of Chuka, ' I gave them my staff. They had been left with nothing, no cattle, no goats, no children, not even the most important of all things, that is rain.' It was by his staff that the Igembe were restored to prosperity.

The custom of the Mugwe sending his staff to some part of his country seems to have been generally observed. The Thagicu beyond the Tana River were informed of any important business, such as war, by messengers who carried the staff of the Mugwe. If warriors moved from one part of the country to the other without carrying this staff they were considered as enemies and attackers. The staff of the Mugwe was a proof that the mission was a peaceful one. Even at present, it is not one of the esoteric insignia of the Mugwe. When I asked to be allowed to take a photograph of M. Mugambi of the Igembe, he

THE MUGWE, A FAILING PROPHET

begged leave to fetch his staff from inside his house and be photographed with it. (But he refused to don his mantle.) So did Muruku, the retired Mugwe of the Igembe; and also M. Ikwenga of the Tigania.

The sacred honey-beer is another insignia of the Mugwe in general. It is used for blessing: the Mugwe sips it and spits it over the faithful. But in a very special way for the Tharaka, the honey-beer is *the* insignia of the Mugwe.[1] There is nothing more valued than the honey-beer preserved by the Mugwe. A very special shrine in the form of a miniature roofed structure is built to keep the sacred honey-beer. It is said and believed that this honey-beer has never failed since the very first Mugwe. Indeed, it cannot be allowed to dry up. It is regarded as the symbol of the continuity and the prosperity of the country. The Mugwe is its custodian and guarantor. It is his duty to see that it does not fail. Struck by the high value attached to this sacred honey, I tried several times to enquire what would be the consequence if, by any unfortunate mischance, the sacred honey should be allowed to dry up or be found to be missing. The elders' reaction was consistently spontaneous and positive: such a thing could not happen. It was only for the sake of the argument that M. Muga of Chokarige was induced to envisage such a contingency: disgrace would certainly fall on the person of the guilty Mugwe, and all the Mugwe's family, as well as the Tharaka, would starve and die in the grip of such a tragic calamity: ' Indeed, no, it was not thinkable! '

Among the Tharaka fees are paid to the Mugwe in the form of honey. No visit to the Mugwe can take place without a measure of honey being paid as an homage.

---

[1] It is significant to note that all through Tharakaland honey is one of the main products. Beeswax is sold by the Tharaka at the markets of the Meru and Kamba. It is also exported to Nairobi.

'BORN TO BE MUGWE'

Honey (a full tin valued at about seventy shillings in the local market) was expressly demanded of me as a fee for being allowed to visit the Mugwe at his residence near Chokarige.

The sacred honey-beer is preserved in a pot or bottle, but no one has access to it without the Mugwe. Even with the Mugwe, the honey-beer is reserved for initiates. M. Ruanda could not consent to my inspecting more closely the sanctuary where the honey-beer was being preserved. It seems, therefore, that the esoteric nature of the things of the Ugwe is also felt among the Tharaka.

Of all the insignia of the Mugwe, the one that has developed as something entirely esoteric is the *kiragu*. There is no possible exact translation of the term into English. In Kimeru it means literally water-reed; but it seems to be derived from the verb *-raga*, to be hidden, and *-ragura*, to divine or uncover the hidden things. No one is supposed to know about the *kiragu*, except the Mugwe. As one elder stated: 'A common man cannot know about *kiragu*. The Mugwe is the one who knows, as a minister of God is the one who knows and teaches about God.'[1] This attitude to *kiragu* is peculiar to the Imenti. Other sub-tribes know the term, but its use is less significant.[2]

M. Ruanda of the Tharaka said that, yes, they have *kiragu*, but their *kiragu* is the honey-beer. Among the Igembe, the term *kiragu* refers to a ritual tree planted at the accession of the new Mugwe. When the new Mugwe of the Igembe is proclaimed, all the elders are gathered at the plain of Ithongoma, on the side-track that stops short of the main road from Maua to Antubociu. It is at Ithongoma that the *kiragu* tree is planted to symbolize the

---

[1] The speaker, M. Arethi M. Twerandu, was an elder of Nkubu where I had been stationed as the Father in charge. He knew me very well and we were good friends.

[2] In current speech the term *Kiragu* may also describe all the paraphernalia of a medicine-man.

102   THE MUGWE, A FAILING PROPHET

power of the newly proclaimed Mugwe. When he dies, his tree is uprooted and burnt at his former house. When I passed through Ithongoma I was shown two *kiragu* trees that had been planted at the accession of M. Mugambi.

Among the Imenti, the usage of the term *kiragu* may be equivocal. It refers to different institutions, though all intimately connected with the office of the Mugwe. It is stated, in any case, that ' *kiragu* is not something of the present, on the contrary it dates back to time immemorial' : *kiragu giki ti kya nandi, ni gya kenya na kenya.* We find in this statement the same attitude as we noted among the Tharaka with regard to the sacred honey-beer. Both *kiragu* and the sacred honey-beer are rooted in the early beginning of Meru history. In fact, in one of the myths of origin ' the man with the *kiragu* ' is the prophet who leads the Meru through the water of Mbwa.

A first meaning of the term *kiragu* refers to the Mugwe's *mwiriga*, i.e. his lineage: *kiragu ni mwiriga jwawe ni ju jwetagwa kiragu*, ' *kiragu* is his lineage, it is that which is called *kiragu* '. The possession and the inheritance of the *kiragu* by one of the Mugwe's lineage gives a sacred character to all the other members. It endows them with some special power, especially in relation to rain, which entitles them to special consideration by other people. Members of the Mugwe's lineage are not supposed to be cut and lose blood. If this happens, rain will come in an abnormal way. When circumcision is performed on boys of this lineage, their loss of blood will cause an extraordinary amount of rain to wash the ground. Whenever there is a sudden fall of rain, one says that some bloody event has happened within that *mwiriga*. It is thus that ' the people from Kirirwa ' (the place of the Mugwe of the Imenti) are greatly feared and respected.

'BORN TO BE MUGWE'

Kiragu can also indicate the sacred person of the Mugwe. Some of my informants stated that the word describes 'a sacred person like a bishop': a connotation that we have already noted as explicitly applied to the Mugwe as such.

By a further extension of the word, perhaps more common, *kiragu* is taken to mean 'a pot', *kiragu ni kongu (kaongo)*. It is the pot in which 'the medicines of every kind', *mithega ya mithemba yonthe*, used by the Mugwe, are contained. The following are said to be 'the medicines': *uuki*, honey; *mwere, ugimbi, munyaki*, all different kinds of millet; *muya*, sorghum; *ncabi*, a black bean; *nkina, mboco, nthoroko*, other kinds of beans; *mpempe*, maize. Though the above list was dictated with some certainty, the elders soon remarked that, really, nobody can know what is contained in the *kiragu*, not even the elders of the Mugwe's lineage, because the *kiragu* cannot be seen by anyone.

Finally, *kiragu* is, generally speaking, the power of the Ugwe, the Ugwe itself or the thing by which the Mugwe is made to be the Mugwe. Consequently at the time of the accession, the *kiragu* is described as the most important of all the insignia of the Mugwe. It is officially entrusted to him, and after that he is not supposed to show it or its contents to anybody. Also, when he carries it in his hand for blessing, he must not let it be seen by anyone. For this reason, the Mugwe of the Imenti was described as keeping his left hand, with which he is supposed to carry the *kiragu*, always under cover of his mantle. Even when he plays draughts, *kiothi*, his left hand must remain covered. There is no doubt that the *kiragu* of the Imenti is considered by those who know and fear the power of the Mugwe as its most sacred symbol. The elders state that it cannot fail, because 'if it finishes it can always be reproduced, in the same way as men die but leave their children to carry on after them'.

104 THE MUGWE, A FAILING PROPHET

The above description of the insignia of the Mugwe has revealed the existence of some measure of secrecy surrounding his office. There are insignia that are shown only to the initiates, and there are other things that are forbidden to the general view. One has to take into account this esoteric element in order to understand the nature and the present position of the Mugwe among the Meru. The stress on secrecy is not of the same degree in all the sub-tribes. The highest degree is found among the Imenti. But here, as we have noted already and as we shall further analyse, the situation is rather involved. There is a possibility of regarding ' the *kiragu* and all that ', as a ' sacramentum ', the secret mystery that holds together Imenti society, at least, in its old form. The idea of a sacred mystery as something necessary to consolidate the structure of a society, is an idea native to the mind of such neighbouring tribes as the Kikuyu.[1] One might be inclined to take the same idea for granted for the Meru also. But, as we have seen, it is only among the Imenti that one can really speak of a secret. With the Imenti there are, as we shall see, other contingent causes, also historical, that may account for their present secrecy about everything Mugwe, and therefore the esoteric character of the Mugwe's office cannot be taken, at least at the present stage of our knowledge, as evidence of a supposed secret character of the Mugwe institution.

[1] The following proverb illustrates the attitude of the Kikuyu on this subject: *Andu matari ndundu mahuraguo na njogoma imwe*, ' People without a secret entente are brought to their knees at a single stroke '.

Chapter Five

THE POWER OF THE MUGWE

I. THE MORAL VIRTUES OF THE MUGWE

' The Ugwe,' said the elders of Chuka, ' is made up of all the actions of the Mugwe: they are very good and beneficial to his people.' The same conception is found among all the other sub-tribes. Though there is no single Mugwe for all the Meru, but one for each of those sub-tribes that were found at the first crossing of Mbwa, yet their power and activity are the same everywhere. Also the expectation of his own people with regard to each Mugwe is the same everywhere. The Mugwe is supposed to foster the general welfare of his people by his blessing and by the goodness of his life. ' The Ugwe is one: to protect the country, to protect the seeds, to help people to live well,' *Ugwe ni bumwe, kumenyerera nthiguru, kumenyerera mbeu, kubanda antu bagakitha bwega.*[1] The man who becomes Mugwe must, therefore, be outstanding for his moral character.

This consideration is brought to bear in a very special measure at the time of the succession to the office. Though the hereditary principle is observed, its application may be qualified in order to select the right candidate, even if this means that the first-born son of the living Mugwe is excluded.

The first requirement for a candidate is that he be *mutheru muno*, ' most pure '. The expression may refer literally to the body of the candidate in the sense that it

---

[1] ' To help people to live well' should be rendered literally: ' So that people may harvest well '.

must be sound, free from all blemish and mutilation; it may also refer to his social status, in the sense that he must be born in the lineage that holds the power of the Ugwe. More frequently it has a definite moral significance with reference to the character of the candidate, and the expression is often heard as *mutheru nkoro*, ' pure of heart ', which means firstly a man of clean heart, i.e. of noble aims, loyal, or of a happy disposition, as opposed to a man of unclean, deceitful heart; and it means also a man free from sin, holy, as we have noted already, comparing the Mugwe to the *ntindiri* elders.

An Igembe elder gave the following summary of the moral virtues that the Mugwe should possess: 1. The Mugwe should be a well born person; 2. He should be a pure man all through his life; 3. He should not kill any animal or any man from his childhood to his death; 4. He should be a man of good character; 5. He should follow the correct ancient customs of the Meru; 6. He should not do anything harmful to his people.

The early training of a candidate, as was noted, is closely supervised by the Mugwe in office and by the candidate's sponsors. The candidate himself must realize that he is born to be the Mugwe, a sacred man, and that therefore he must distinguish himself by living up to the optimum pattern of moral and social life. After his initiation, besides being instructed like all the other initiates on how to behave as a man, he is also told that his station in life is not like the others. Other initiates may show off their strength as befits them and may also go after girls; the young candidate must restrain himself and be continent ' for there is no need for him to show that he has the force of a *muthaka*, a young initiate '. He should likewise not be aggressive, and his honesty should be above reproach. The arrangements for his marriage are

THE POWER OF THE MUGWE 107

settled between his father, the elders of his family, and the father and elders of the girl's family.

In married life the Mugwe is also supposed to conduct himself in an outstanding and singular way. His behaviour is indeed a matter of wonder to all. ' The Mugwe,' stated an Imenti elder, ' is a very good man, pure in heart, whose actions are also pure. He cannot do anything evil to his people. If you are married, you may think of your wife, but the Mugwe does not do so. He cannot go to his wife and say he wants to have a child. He himself states that if he wants to be good he could not please himself by following a different way of life, otherwise God would not regard him as a good leader. For the same reason, no outside woman can ever have intercourse with him.' And another elder from Imenti added: ' Another wonder for common people: the Mugwe never asks for his wife; it is his wife who asks for him. When his wife was still a girl, she was informed about this by the elders and other women. The Mugwe can abstain for years.' Continence is imperative whenever there is to be a sacrifice or special prayers to God.

The Mugwe is also expected to keep sober. He can, of course, drink fermented beverages, but he must not be addicted to them. For the same reason, he is not supposed to go around casually and join beer-parties. Drunkenness is a rather common fault among the elders: not so with the Mugwe.

With regard to this particular point, it is of interest to record here an episode in illustration. It was narrated by M. Ajore, a very old man of Kiramana age-class, from Imenti.

Once I invited the Mugwe to my house. He came and we drank much, but he did not become drunk (*atiogitaga*). The reason why he did not want to become drunk was his fear of

108 THE MUGWE, A FAILING PROPHET

letting his mantle fall down. When he left my place to return home, he arrived at Kajeri, and there he fell under a tree. So a very big sheep was brought and killed on the spot. Some fat was smeared on him, some was poured on the ground. The next morning, he asked me: 'What have you done? Will you do so again, my *muthoni* [lit. my kinsman, or friend]?' 'No, I will not, and it was not my fault, my *muthoni*.' But he said, 'You can call me again, because you, my *muthoni*, have got many things and you know how to do the things of the elderhood, *mantu ja ukuru*.'

The last expression *mantu ja ukuru*, the things of the elderhood, needs explaining. It means first the material making of wine which it is the elders' privilege to drink in parties. It means also, and primarily, the behaviour, the care, the respect, that must be shown to the elders in every circumstance. The host in the above episode had acted properly towards the Mugwe, being scrupulous in offering an expiating sacrifice for the fallen old man. Having shown how he knew the way of the elders, the Mugwe is indulgent with him and says that he may invite him again.

The episode is also significant from another point of view. The intoxicated Mugwe indicates that all the high requirements of his moral life set an ideal to which the Mugwe should conform. In practice he may fall short of that ideal, and for that he makes amends by offering sacrifices.

The Mugwe is also supposed to be a strict observer of the old customs. The present state of decadence of the old way of life was not favourable to my research on this point, though I was lucky to be unexpectedly confronted by some significant pieces of evidence. Thus, one morning, I visited M. Ruanda of the Tharaka: he was engaged in building a new house for himself and his family. While

THE POWER OF THE MUGWE

conversing with him, I was struck by a small gourd cap under a tiny bush, the only plant that had been left in the area of the new house. On my enquiring, I discovered that in the early morning, before work, M. Ruanda had offered a libation to his ancestors as a propitiation for the new residence, showing how exact he had been in keeping this old custom that very few Meru now observe.

The Mugwe must be kind to his people, and to everybody else, even to enemies. Examples are given of his good behaviour towards prisoners of war, i.e. strangers who had been caught with their arms in the territory of the Meru; he gave them food, which he also supplied when he let them go free. When young men were away on a raid, the Mugwe was always 'thinking' of them, and this was sufficient to ensure their victory. The goodness of the Mugwe is, to some extent, proverbial. Among the Tharaka I found that the name Mugwe had been given to a poor disabled man, incapable of doing any harm. I was also told that if a small child behaves very politely, he may be called *Kagwe* for compliment, as if to say 'he looks like a little Mugwe'.

One cannot help asking why and how the Mugwe could be expected to live such a chaste, sober, and good life. When I put a similar question to M. Kiganka of the Chuka, this was his answer: 'Because the Mugwe represents all his country, like the King'! In other words, the Mugwe stands for the welfare of his society, its safety, its continuity, its integrity. No ordinary man living a common life would be considered as suitable for such a high office. No ordinary man would find himself in a position to secure God's blessing for his people. Indeed, the relationship between the Mugwe and God is a very close one as we shall analyse further on,

110 THE MUGWE, A FAILING PROPHET

2. THE BLESSING OF THE MUGWE

The rite of blessing consisted usually in sipping a mouthful of honey-beer and gently spitting it on to the people. The rite was observed by the Mugwe, but it is not really different from the old mode of salutation observed by the elders. A similar form of greeting by an elder was always an expression of esteem and of special love. This rite could be performed on its own, or it could conclude a prayer, or open a sacrificial ritual at which a beast was killed.

A very special power in connection with the blessings of the Mugwe was popularly attributed to his left hand. It is the hand, as we saw, that the Mugwe always keeps under his mantle, it is the hand with which he holds the *kiragu*, even when playing. Anyone going to him was first advised by the elders to be respectful and modest when facing the Mugwe, but above all never to dare to look at his left hand. In that hand, it was thought, the Mugwe holds the power of his blessing: it was enough for him to lift that hand in order to stop any enemy attacking his people. This belief was common with the Tharaka, the Chuka, the Igembe and the Imenti; but it is especially with the Imenti that the left hand of the Mugwe has become a source of great awe.

There were several occasions, all of general importance to the whole country, when the blessings of the Mugwe were asked for. This, in fact, is a distinguishing mark of the blessing activity of the Mugwe. The Mugwe could not be concerned with individuals as such and their petty problems. In some special instances, because he was kind, he took care to bless individuals, such as pregnant women or the poor, but even these personal cases reflected the general welfare of his country. No other events were of greater interest in that sense than the opening of an

THE POWER OF THE MUGWE 111

initiation period, the training of the young initiates in the *gaaru*, and the formation of a new age-class at the performance of the *ntuiko*. And these, indeed, were the main occasions when the Mugwe came out to give his blessing in his full attire.

The opening of an initiation period was marked by the blessing of the circumciser's knife by the Mugwe. The custom was very probably universal among the Meru in the past. Nowadays, I found that it still obtains with the Tharaka. The circumciser, or *mutani*, of the Tharaka is now a very old man, Nkeya by name. At every season, before any candidate for initiation is operated on, Nkeya pays an official visit to M. Ruanda, the Mugwe, and takes to him his own knife and the knives of the two other circumcisers of the Tharaka, who work under his control. The Mugwe blesses the knives, and only after that can circumcision be celebrated anywhere. For the occasion, Nkeya pays a fee of a ram to the Mugwe.

The training of the initiates in the *gaaru* was in some measure controlled and blessed by the Mugwe. During their period in the *gaaru*, the Mugwe used to visit them, and he could stay with them explaining the old customs of the Meru, and advise them on their plans for raids or for defence. His interest could go as far as making certain about their food and seeing that they were properly fed. Generally it is said that the Mugwe blessed the warriors before their raids and gave them ' medicines ' (*mithega*). Among the Tharaka the powerful blessing by Mutuampea is remembered and the medicines he gave to the young warriors. The blessing consisted of mixing all sorts of seeds in a pot, in a way similar to that described by the Imenti elders with regard to the *kiragu*, and with that mixture made sacred by the saliva of the Mugwe, Mutuampea sprinkled the warriors. To every one of them he gave also

112   THE MUGWE, A FAILING PROPHET

some short sticks to throw as a first arm of protection against the enemy.

The following is a formula of blessing used by the Mugwe of the Tharaka when visiting the *gaaru*. It was dictated by M. Kamunde, a very intelligent and reliable old man:

Buragia intu	May you have things. Increase your
Mburi, ng'ombe,	Goats, cattle,
Mwere, uuki;	Millet, honey;
na uria ati na biu	and if one has not them
na we agee.	let him have.

The *ntuiko*, as we know, was only performed under the authority of the Mugwe. The blessing that took place at the event was described thus by an elder of the Imenti: 'When a new *nthuki*, age-class, was taken to the field (*ikumagarua kyenine*), women were allowed to come only for bringing food to their children. No man was allowed to speak when on the field: only the Mugwe did so. He shouted very clearly to make people hear what he was saying. His prayers were always merciful (*jari ja kiao*), and they were concerned with (the welfare of) the country and of the people.' Such a solemn ritual was, more or less, observed by all the sub-tribes.

The following formulæ may be taken as typical of the prayers made by the Mugwe in blessing. They are not fixed texts consistently followed, nor are they couched in a special liturgical language, though some archaic words may be detected. Prayers are generally *ex impromptu*, but they tend to conform to a standardized pattern.

The first formula was recorded among the Tharaka. It is a type of litany, in which the leader is the Mugwe to whom the chorus answers.

3. M. Lunyiru, the diviner of the Igembe. See pages 33 and 132.

4. M. Kamunde, with all his professional tools. Notice the structure in the background to protect M. Kamunde's professional bag. See page 43.

THE POWER OF THE MUGWE 113

Thathaia, Murungu:	Chorus:	Thai,	Let us pray God:	pray,
mburi,		thai,	for goats:	pray,
ng'ombe,		thai,	for cattle:	pray,
rwana,		thai,	for children:	pray,
Thathaia, Murungu,		thai.	Let us pray God:	pray.

Guthathaia, from which also comes the sound *thai*, is certainly an archaic term. It is very similar to the Kikuyu *guthaithai* which was the proper word for praying to Ngai, God, and never used for propitiating the ancestors' spirits.

The next formula is not a litany. It comes also from the Tharaka and was dictated by M. Kamunde. The speaker is the Mugwe who prays for the young warriors:

Ee, ee, ibendwe, ee, ibonthe,	Ehe, ehe, may they be loved, ehe, by all,
baciare, bwithe (baithe?), na bang'ina	may they beget, fathers and mothers,
bagite mburi, ng'ombe,	may they have goats and cattle,
baciare aana babaingi muno.	may they beget children very many.

One may note how in these prayers the young warriors are wished fruitful issues both of children and of herds. The continuity of his people constitutes the main interest of the Mugwe.

The welfare of the country and the people is at stake when a period of drought is so prolonged that there is fear of famine and starvation. The power of the Mugwe is therefore sought. In ordinary circumstances, praying for rain is a matter that may concern any elder. He may offer the sacrifice of a goat or sheep either for his lineage or for the whole of his clan. The Mugwe is greater than an ordinary elder, and his power extends beyond the limits of a single clan, even his own. What the Mugwe does, he does for the whole of the country.

The ritual followed in praying for rain may be very

THE MUGWE, A FAILING PROPHET

elaborate as, for instance, among the Tigania. When the drought becomes really serious, the Mugwe or the Mukiama, each in his own area, performs a special sacrifice. This must take place in a sacred grove or forest. The Mugwe leads a procession to this place, headed by a sheep. In fact, it is this sacrificial sheep that is supposed to lead the way to discover a pool inside the grove. When the pool is found, the sheep is offered on the spot and the Mugwe blesses the country and prays:

Murungu, tukurumbaga, ututethie.	Murungu, we pray, help us.
Tutuure, turi na inya,	That we may live, have strength,
tugie twana, na ng'ombe,	May we bear children, and cattle,
na baria bari natu,	And those who have them,
nabo bakauga:	They too say:
Utethie twana twetu.	Help our children.

The water of the pool in the forest is generally covered by water-lilies and similar water plants. It is said that if, during the Mugwe's prayer, the leaves part so that the water is visible, the omen for the coming of the rain is very good. If, after this first sacrifice, the rain still fails, the procession to the forest will be renewed, and this time the Mugwe is joined in his prayer by a small innocent girl.[1]

Among the other sub-tribes the Mugwe went around the country blessing and praying for the rain. Thus, among the Imenti, I recorded a description of an itinerary followed by the Mugwe on a similar occasion. 'These are the places (*biuruku*) where he used to rest when he was going out to bless. From Kirirwa he stopped first at Karinga ka Mbugi; from there he went to Muringa jwa Munguma;

---

[1] The daughter of M. Ikwenga, the old Mugwe of the Igoki-Tigania, accompanied her father to the forest. I spoke to the child, now an educated girl, and she described how she went dressed in a skin cloth, *nguo ya miguta.*

THE POWER OF THE MUGWE 115

and then to Kyoroni where there was a big tree (*muringa*).
On his way he was met by the elders who would ask him
to offer (kill) the goat of the rain (*mburi ya ngai*). Having
blessed them, he returned by the same road and he did
not want to return by any other road. Having returned,
he rested again.'

The following is a formula used by the Mugwe of the
Imenti in blessing:

Kirinyaga, mwene into bionthe,	Kirinyaga, owner of all things,
ndakuthaitha, umpe mabatara jakwa	I pray Thee, give me what I need,
ni untu ndi na thina,	because I am suffering,
na antu bakwa,	and also my children (are suffering)
na into bionthe biria biri	and all the things that are
nthiguru iji yakwa.	in this country of mine.
Ndakuromba utuuro,	I beg Thee for life,
buria bwega buri na into,	the good one with things (rich life)
antu babega bati murimu,	healthy people with no disease,
bakuciara rwana rurwega.	may they bear healthy children.
Na kinya aka baria barikitie	And also to women who suffer
kuthata, uingure njira tu	because they are barren, open the way
iu bone twana.	by which they may see children.
Mburi, ng'ombe, irio, mauuki.	(Give) goats, cattle, food, honey.
Na kinya mathina ja ntere ingi	And also the troubles of the other lands
iria ntikumenya, urite.	that I do not know, remove.

The above prayer is addressed to God, *Kirinyaga*, whose
abode is on Mount Kenya, the mountain of brightness;
God: the possessor of brightness. A point of particular
interest to note is the reference to ' the other lands ' whose
troubles the Mugwe does not know at that moment.
These other lands are the other parts of his own country,

116   THE MUGWE, A FAILING PROPHET

for which he also prays, not only for the one in which he finds himself at the time of the prayer. The reference is significant as evidence of the Mugwe's outside commitments and interests.

This point needs emphasizing because it helps us to understand correctly the nature of the Mugwe and to avoid possible misconceptions. Though the Mugwe may be asked to, and in fact does, pray for rain, he is not a rain-maker in the usual meaning of the term, viz. he is not a practitioner who has learnt the tricks of the trade for causing rain and who makes a living out of them. Rain is for the Mugwe just one further thing necessary to secure the welfare of his country and avoid disaster to his people.

Another aspect of the Mugwe's capacity to bless is described in relation to 'the poor'. An instance occurs, according to my informants, when a man, who wants to get married, meets with difficulties in gathering the necessary amount of cattle and honey for his bridewealth. 'The poor' may, thus, approach the Mugwe and ask for his blessing. The way this blessing is given is very illuminating. The Mugwe can help 'the poor' by advice and by prayer. The following may be the content of the Mugwe's advice:

Go, cut a bee-hive so that you may get honey. With that honey you will be able to buy goats. Till your shamba and get some crop and no one will abuse you when you ask for food. Get plenty of millet, but give some to the birds. Get plenty of honey, but give some to *mathegiri* or the honey-sucker beast. Do all this, and *Mwene-inya* [i.e. the Possessor of strength, or Almighty God] will also give you.

The advice of the Mugwe may also be couched in a prayer formula, as the following one by the Mugwe of the Tharaka:

THE POWER OF THE MUGWE

Jukia murua, ukarime.	Take your digging stick, cultivate.
Jukia kibanga, ugacae miatu	Take your cutlass and cut some hives
ni kinda ugia uuki.	so that you may get honey
Na uuki buu nabu ugure mburi	With that honey buy goats,
mburi iji ni iciarage tuburi	those goats will bring forth two
twiri kana maatha maatha.	kids or by twins.

The next formula was recorded among the Imenti; it is a prayer by the Mugwe:

Mwene-inya, mbigirwe kiao.	Almighty God, have mercy on me.
Kaana gaka gakwa kone into bibi	May this child of mine see these things,
ni kenda ngugi yakwa	so that my work
yoneke kiri antu bonthe	may be seen by all men,
na kinya baria batimbitikagia,	and also those who do not trust me,
nyanyo yabo igaruke.	may their infidelity change.

Labour, thrift, and generosity are, thus, the conditions on which the blessing of the Mugwe to ' the poor ' is made to depend. Thrift by which ' the poor ' can help themselves is suggested in a very practical, though naïve, way, while laziness and begging for food are clearly, though indirectly, condemned (' do your work, in order not to be abused! '). The suggestion to give some share of the crop to the birds and some honey to the honey-sucker is significant. There is no special evidence to support the interpretation of such offerings as a kind of first-fruits sacrifice, though reference to this type of offering in the advice of the Mugwe does certainly invite a similar interpretation. Only if these conditions are fulfilled is God, in His attribute as the Almighty, invoked to bless.

The social significance of the blessing of ' the poor '

118 THE MUGWE, A FAILING PROPHET

should be stressed. They are generally despised and are, in any case, social outcasts. It is typical in this respect that the poor man is refused assistance by the ordinary man in getting his bridewealth. The blessing of the Mugwe is meant to restore such a man to his own society and to sponsor, as it were, his re-integration into the elders' assemblies.

The blessing of the Mugwe was also sought by pregnant or barren women. He advised the latter to go and look after cattle (work usually restricted to men) and to observe their ways, so that by seeing their intercourse they could derive impressions which would excite them to conceive. Pregnant women were asked to drink *mwonyo* or natural soda water; to wash their backs with it so that they might gain strength and bear without trouble. In some sections of Meru the blessing of pregnant women by the Mugwe was held to be essential. It is told of an old woman of the Imenti, that while she was young and pregnant, she did not go to be blessed by the Mugwe; it happened that all her children died, and she became a sorcerer, i.e. a poisoner and a despised creature. The fertility of women is essential for the continuity of a people, and this is the obvious reason why the Mugwe was asked to extend his blessing to women individually.

3. THE SANCTIONS AND CURSES OF THE MUGWE

As we have noted, the greatness of such an extraordinary being as the Mugwe is a cause of awe and wonder to the ordinary man. But though the Mugwe is therefore very highly respected and obeyed, such respect and obedience would not be so absolute if there were not sanctions or fear of some automatic punishment, to counteract the human tendency to disobedience. Indeed, the most powerful sanction is the certainty of future failure or

THE POWER OF THE MUGWE 119

disgrace if one should dare to resist the Mugwe. The consequence of disrespect and disobedience to the Mugwe was always described by my informants in terms of death, loss of one's children, destruction of one's family, or disaster for the whole country.[1]

If the warriors should fail to go to the Mugwe and be blessed before any of their raids, failure and destruction, either by wild animals on their way or by their enemies, will surely await them. We have noted before, how the Mugwe always 'thinks' of the warriors while they are out on an expedition. The presence of the Mugwe among his people is essential for their welfare; but his removal entails disaster for all. Typical in this respect is the reference by M. Kiganka of the Chuka to his forced removal from his fields to the new village of Chera at the time when all the Chuka were forced to 'villagize' on account of the Mau Mau rebellion. M. Kiganka commented: 'The Mugwe cannot be removed from his house. If he is, it would be like destroying his own people. This of Mau Mau is an example.'

The sanction of the Mugwe was also sought to confirm a sentence passed by the council of elders, even the *njuri*. Thus, I was told by an Igembe elder, if a man had been found guilty and condemned to die by the elders, he could find asylum at the house of the Mugwe, in which case the verdict of the Mugwe, whether favourable or not, was considered as final in either case.

The blessing of the Mugwe to close a dispute was regarded as a sanction, and therefore to be highly respected. Among the Tharaka, I was taken one day by M. Kamundi to a stone in a field not far from his house.

---

[1] M. Ruanda explained the dual divisions of the Tharaka, Urio and Umotho, as a punishment by the first Mugwe. Those of Urio were grumbling, and therefore the Mugwe separated them from those of Umotho who being 'loyal to him were surely his children'.

120   THE MUGWE, A FAILING PROPHET

The stone had been set there and blessed by Mutuampea, the great Mugwe, as a sign of settlement in a dispute over this land. When I asked M. Kamundi to point to the stone with his finger because I wanted a photograph of him in that position, he flatly refused, saying that he would certainly die if he did so 'because the stone had been blessed by the Mugwe'. He agreed, however, to be photographed standing near the stone. It was not a very large stone, of no special appearance, and it certainly could not have been identified by any uninformed person.

We have seen how much respect and fear there was for the left hand of the Mugwe: no one might see it or look on it without dying. Similar respect was also shown for the residence of the Mugwe. People generally, except his family or the elders of his clan and age, did not go near it. No one, in any case, was allowed to approach the house of the Mugwe with his spear or sword, or wearing sandals. When the Mugwe had crossed a river, the place where he crossed was named *iriuku ria Mugwe* or the wading place of the Mugwe. No one, not even cattle, was allowed to cross there after that. Among the Imenti, if the Mugwe happened to spend a night in a house not his own, that house must be burnt down; for this reason he always preferred to spend the night inside a sacred grove, which was forbidden to an ordinary man. (Such groves are still noticeable in many parts of the country throughout Meru District.) The reason stated for the above prohibitions was to prevent evil attacks by poisoners or other enemies.

All the wrath of the Mugwe fell on recalcitrant thieves when the case was considered hopeless. Among the Imenti, the Mugwe, in such a case, would ask for some grass from the criminal's house. He would then burn the grass, and say: *mucii juu jukathira ta nyaki iji,* 'this

THE POWER OF THE MUGWE

house shall finish like this grass'. Some of my Tharaka informants stated that the Mugwe changed the thief into a wild beast, a leopard, or similar animal. In that condition, the thief was forced to take some goats to the house of the Mugwe to pay for his crimes. Afterwards, the Mugwe would allow him to resume his human form.

A more common sanction by the Mugwe of the Tharaka when a theft was reported to him, was to take a bow or another stick, break it, and spell his curse over the thief who would certainly die after that.

A very similar sanction and curse were reserved by the Mugwe of the Imenti for a 'girl with child while still in the house of her father ', and for her lover. He would demand grass from their houses, burn it and say: ' May they be destroyed like this grass '; he would then take a bow, break it, and say: ' May they be broken like this bow.'

The cursing power of the Mugwe is well expressed in an elaborate invocation which I recorded from an elder of Kithuri clan, the clan of the Tharaka Mugwe.

Antu ibabue, antu ibabue,	May people be well, may they be well,
baithe, bang'ina,	male, female,
baithe, bang'ina,	male, female,
mburi, ng'ombe	goats, cattle,
twiji, twari,	boys and girls,
baunganie mitwe.	may they multiply themselves (lit. heads).
Ncai inu ituthame.	Bad luck go away from us.
Mwiji uria uthuraga ungi,	The (uncircumcised) man who hates another,
arora.	may he perish.
Uria uthuraga antu ba bakwa,	Who hates these people of mine,
arora.	may he perish.
Muntu uria weagia,	The man who does wrong
nawe arora.	may he also perish.

Muntu uria uthuraga ungi	The man who curses another,
akauga: ' arora ',	who says: ' may he perish ',
atiramira kuria ruo	he will die on the spot cursed with
rogutiramira	the curse of the back.

' Cursed with the curse of the back ' refers to a vulgar gesture, generally made by quarelling women, by which the anus is shown in contempt to the adversary. In the above cursing, the Mugwe strikes at two of the most perverse sins: the hatred of man for man and the abuse of sex. Both constitute an omnipresent menace to the essence of society which is based on mutual understanding and co-operation. It befits the Mugwe, therefore, to condemn them both as strongly as possible. Thus, though cursing may appear to contradict the exalted mildness of the Mugwe, it emphasizes his responsibility for the welfare of his people.

4. THE MUGWE AS JUDGE

Sometimes the Mugwe is described as a judge. We have noted already that a sentenced man had the right of appeal to him and could find asylum at his house. Mutuampea of the Tharaka is still remembered as a great judge. An elder of the Imenti stated that the Mugwe was a judge ' like the judges of the Europeans '. And the same man went on to explain what he meant: ' The Mugwe,' he said, ' thinks before he speaks. He is not quick in his opinion, but he evaluates all the pros and cons of the case, in the meanwhile keeping the contendents to the point and attentive to his own words. His judgments were always, therefore, good. But his people tried to settle things by themselves in order to save him trouble.'

The last remark by this Imenti elder is much to the point and helps us to understand better the function of the

THE POWER OF THE MUGWE 123

Mugwe in this respect. In fact, trying and discussing cases was not really part of the Mugwe's peculiar office; that was the right and duty of the elders as such, who are formed into councils for that purpose. The action of the Mugwe and his arbitration were sought only when a supernatural sanction was felt to be needed. In any case, the word of the Mugwe was always final.

5. ' THE UGWE IS FROM GOD '

An aspect of the power of the Mugwe that needs to be more fully analysed is his position with relation to God.

There are two names by which the Meru refer to God, *Murungu*, and *Ngai*. Murungu is the old Bantu term, and is commonly used by all the Meru sub-tribes. Ngai is a word borrowed from the Masai, and while among the Kikuyu it has come to be the only name for God, among the Meru it is not often heard, and then more among the Tharaka and the Igembe than among the other sub-tribes. The idea of God for the Meru is not a very clear one; they take for granted the presence of God in the world, something self-evident, that one does not discuss: He is there, that is all. He is thought of as the Almighty, the All-seer, the All-giver, who is good, the Master of life and death. He is certainly considered as the Creator of all things and of man; but the Meru have no idea whatsoever how creation was carried out. In everyday life, God may be honoured by prayers and sacrifices. Though to a superficial observer the Meru might appear religiously indifferent, a careful researcher can easily discover men of deep religious feeling who care for God and pray to Him even daily. One such man was my old friend M. Kamunde of Chokarige. This man had the habit of prayer, and his heavy lot in life was relieved by his frequent appeals to God. The following is a series of prayers that I recorded

124 THE MUGWE, A FAILING PROPHET

from M. Kamunde; they may give some indication of how much God means to the Meru:

Ngai, ni gwe wambombire	Ngai, you created me
na ni gwe umbikerete inya.	and you gave me strength.
Gantu karia kari konthe	Every little thing in its entirety
ni ka Ngai.	is of Ngai.
Umbikere inya,	Instil strength into me,
unenkere into bionthe:	give me all things:
mwere, muya, nthoroko, na mburi	millet, sorghum, beans, goats
na ng'ondu.	and lambs.
Umenyere ntikathi kararo kamwe	Guard me from going to any resting
na nkoma,	place with (bad) spirits,
ni untu nkoma imbee ni cio cietaga	because bad spirits are they who call (trouble)
muntu amami.	a sleeping man.

A prayer in the evening:

Ngai, ni gwe Munene, ntethia bwega,	Ngai, you are the Lord, help me well.
ni kenda ngoka ruu	So that I may get up tomorrow
marungu jethera jageri	with my limbs healthy
na umbonie ngugi iria nthithia.	and show me the work I have to do.

A prayer before work:

Ngai, ntethia ni kenda ntiona ugwati	Ngai, help me that I do not see any danger
nkirita ngugi,	while I work,
ni untu ni nkumenya	because I know
kuri ugwati bubwinge.	that there is many a danger.

Another prayer:

Murungu, ni gwe wombire antu	Murungu, you created men
na ni gwe wombire irungu bionthe	and you created all the members

THE POWER OF THE MUGWE

bia mwere. Aromba kanywa, nyoro,	of the body. He created the mouth
mitho, na mugongo.	the nose, the eyes, and the back.
Na ni gwe wombire nyamo cionthe.	And you created all the animals.
Aromba aromba kinya iniore riti mutiro.	He creates even the monkey without a tail.

The above are examples of prayers to God from an individual. There are other instances when God is invoked and prayed to by a whole community, be it a family or a clan or the whole sub-tribe. On such communal occasions, sacrifices of sheep or goats are offered to God, whose help is invoked because it is felt that only His almighty assistance can bring relief or sanction the event. Similar instances are calamities such as a drought or an epidemic or events such as marriage or a death, and they are always of a general character affecting the well-being of the whole sub-tribe.

In the everyday life of the individual, the presence of the spirits of the ancestors is much more felt than the presence of God. The spirits are honoured as such, but prayers are addressed to them in order to placate them and keep them away. Everything that goes wrong, every disease, or every mishap, provided it befalls a single person or a single family, is considered to be the result of an offended spirit. Only when the event is of sufficient magnitude (like being struck by lightning) is it thought that God may have been its cause. It happens, thus, that invocations to the spirits are most frequently heard on the lips of the ordinary man, and the prayer is generally couched in the following terms: *Nkoma cia cucu (juju), ntethieni,* 'spirits of my ancestors, assist me'.

The evidence above shows how much the supernatural is felt in everyday life by the Meru. Therefore it is not

126 THE MUGWE, A FAILING PROPHET

surprising to find that the personality of the Mugwe, with such extraordinary power and singular moral virtues, is thought to be specially related to God. Indeed the relationship of the Mugwe to God is a very close one. We noted already how the Ugwe is said to derive directly from God. The Mugwe is, thus, the representative of God. Of the Mukiama of the Tigania, one elder stated that *ni mutome kiri Ngai*, he is the messenger of God. The Mugwe is ' selected by Ngai ', *mukuru muthure ni Ngai*.

The office of the Mugwe is also described more boldly when the Mugwe is actually called God. It was with great surprise and the utmost interest that I first recorded a similar expression from the present chief of the Tharaka. Afterwards, I was to find that the description was universal and accepted by all the Meru elders. The following statement dictated to me by Kaboto M. Arethi, an elder of Murungi age-class of the Imenti, Nkomari, indicates clearly the veneration of the elders for the Mugwe in this sense:

We akari ja Murungu, na mantu	He is like God, and all his things
jawe jonthe ni jonanagia ati we ni muntu ari utheru bwa nkoro ti ja antu bange. Kuringana na jau jonthe gutiwe otamukiraga.	show that he is pure of heart not like the other men. According to all these things there is none who does not respect him.
Antu ni bendaga kinya kuuga ni jawe Ithe wao kana ni jawe Ngai wao. Gitumi ni mantu jawe jona-nagia ati we ni muntu mwanya muno na bange.	Men go as far as saying that he is their father or their God. The reason is that his things show that he is a man very different from the others.

Other similar statements were also recorded: ' Mugwe is our God. He is called God because of all his good deeds

THE POWER OF THE MUGWE   127

for his people.' 'The Mugwe, don't we call him our God?' When I enquired of M. Kamunde the true meaning of these and other similar statements, he replied: 'It is not that he is our God, but his words are so good that they are always blessed by God.'

There is no question, therefore, of divinity being attributed to the Mugwe; he is not an incarnation of God, nor even a divine king. The statements by the elders leave no doubt and make any misinterpretation impossible on this point. Nor is there any evidence whatsoever that the high regard by which the Mugwe can be compared to God was ever sought by the Agwe themselves in order to satisfy their own ambitions for power and prestige. It is the idea of the Ugwe as a power that comes from God that is responsible for this attitude of the elders towards the Mugwe.

The relationship of the Mugwe to God is also illustrated by the way he prays at his blessings. In all his prayers the Mugwe addresses himself to God, never to the spirits of the ancestors. *Murungu, Kirinyaga, Mwene into bionthe*, are all terms used only and always for God. It is to God Almighty that he prays for his people and their well-being; it is to Him that he represents their needs. This is a distinction to be noted, and it confirms what we have repeatedly remarked, namely, that the Mugwe acts for the welfare of his people as a whole, rather than for the individual. The Mugwe may, of course, pray to the spirits of the ancestors in a private capacity and as a private individual. We observed that with regard to M. Ruanda of the Tharaka. But he never prays to the spirits in his official performances. We can say, therefore, that the Mugwe is not a priest of an ancestor cult. In fact I never heard any of the elders describing him or his office in a way that could support this opinion. On the

128 THE MUGWE, A FAILING PROPHET

contrary, as has been noted, they explicitly called him the representative of God among his people, or the messenger of his people to God.

6. THE MUGWE AND THE *MUGAA*

A common figure in the everyday life of the Meru is their medicine-man. He is known as the *mugaa*, pl. *agaa* (this term, especially among the Tharaka, is also heard as *mugao*, pl. *agao*). A *mugaa* is a practitioner, a doctor, who knows all the answers when a man is sick. His job is to prepare medicines and prescribe them on request. He is paid fees for his assistance. Now we have already recorded how the Mugwe is sometimes described as a man who makes medicines, *mithega*, who keeps the medicines of the tribe, who distributes medicines. The contents of *kiragu* are known generally as *mithega* and the term *mithega* can also be applied to the *kiragu* as such. The Tharaka call the sacred honey-beer *mithega*. When warriors go for a raid, they are blessed by the Mugwe and are supposed to receive from him some special medicine to render them invulnerable. All these facts might be considered as evidence that the Mugwe is a practitioner just as much as an ordinary *mugaa*, though, perhaps, of a higher rank. It is important, therefore, to study wherein lies the difference between the two men.

The first difference is suggested by the description of the Mugwe as the keeper of the medicines of the tribe and of the country, *mithega ya antu bonthe na ya borori*, or, in other words, the Mugwe's concern for the whole of his country and the whole of his people. For that reason, there is only one Mugwe for the whole of a Meru sub-tribe. On the other hand, there can be as many *agaa* as there is demand for them. The *mugaa* is consulted by individuals for individuals and he goes from house to house to visit his clients.

THE POWER OF THE MUGWE

M. Kamunde of Chokarige, himself a *mugaa* and a most reliable informant, described the difference between the two as follows: ' The *mugaa* has to be trained by another *mugaa* and must be given the horn. The Mugwe is born as such from within his lineage, for there is only one Mugwe, while the *agaa* are many. The work of a *mugaa* is to go and visit a man when he is sick, but the Mugwe does not do such a thing. When a *mugaa* treats a sick man he has to pray Nyaga (the same word as Kirinyaga, God). We pray and we say:

Nyaga, tethia muntu uju abwe	Nyaga help this man that he may be well
agagokia ruu	that he may recover tomorrow,
na gwe wende utethie muntu uju abue	and may you want to help this man to be well
wakuruka ou ukurukete	and as overcoming you overcame,
kuruka ma mirigu iji yonthe;	overcome all these troubles
na umbigerwe kyao	and have mercy on me,
ni untu tutije kuromba Murungu	because we do not know how to pray to Murungu
iauria tukuuga nandi.	(differently) from what we say now.'

If the content of the above prayer is compared with the content of that of the Mugwe (see p. 117), one point of difference is evident: the prayers of the Mugwe are all concerned with the general well-being, and consider the prosperity and the continuity of his people. Even when the Mugwe blesses the young initiates or the poor man, his prayer is not limited by the individual needs of the beggar but goes beyond them and becomes of more general application. To the warriors: 'May they beget children very many'; he thinks of the continuity of his people. To the

130   THE MUGWE, A FAILING PROPHET

poor: 'So that my work may be seen *by all men.*' In the prayers by the *mugaa* we find no concern other than for the individual sick man for whom he prays directly at that moment.

The power of the *mugaa* is a technique, or at best an art, which can be acquired by training under the supervision of an experienced *mugaa*. The apprentice will be shown the secrets of the medicines, how to mix the herbs and the powders; how and when to administer them; how to pray. At the end of his training, he will be given the horn, *rugoji*, for storing all the ingredients. The bag of a famous *mugaa* is rich in horns because he knows all the medicines. The Mugwe cannot take hold of the horn, *atyomba kugwata rugoji*: the power of the Mugwe cannot be acquired, it must be inherited.

The Mugwe is above all the *agaa*, and none of these can enter the house of the Mugwe nor can the Mugwe be treated by them. On the contrary, the Mugwe as their chief and the chief of the people has power to summon the *agaa* and give them instructions. Among the Imenti, I was told, when there was an epidemic the elders went to visit the Mugwe. The Mugwe then summoned all the *agaa*, (*ni etaga agaa bakeja*, 'he called all the medicine-men to come') and gave them orders to collect special herbs and prepare special medicines. He himself then blessed the medicines and finally instructed the *agaa* to administer them to the sick.

Because of these relations between the Mugwe and the *agaa*, it would not be surprising if in everyday language the difference between the two powers, of the Ugwe and of the Ugaa, were not always perceived or stressed. I must add, however, that very few of my informants used the term Mugwe and Mugaa indiscriminately, and they were never elders of intelligence and well versed in

THE POWER OF THE MUGWE 131

the local lore. In any case, it seems that the evidence recorded above is sufficient to establish that the Mugwe cannot be properly called, and that he is not, a *mugaa* or medicine-man: there is an essential difference between a public officer and dignitary such as the Mugwe, and a private practitioner such as the *mugaa*.

7. THE MUGWE AND HIS DIVINING ACTIVITY

A problem analogous to the one we have just considered is the difference between the Mugwe and the diviner, *kiruria*. A diviner is a man who has visions and dreams and who foretells the future. Diviners are known to have existed in the past; some are still to be found among the Meru, as well as among other neighbouring tribes, such as the Kikuyu and the Kamba. They attained fame and prestige through the success of their charms and the accuracy of their predictions, for which they were greatly honoured and widely consulted.

Dreaming and divining have also been described as additional powers of the Mugwe. A Tharaka elder attributed exclusively powers of this nature to the first Mugwe: ' He was a dreamer, not a leader. When he had had a dream he was able to say what would happen in the future '. This statement suggests that the divining aspect should be considered. But the assertion that he is not, or was not a leader, is contradicted by the weight of the evidence on the Mugwe's activity. That he acted as a diviner, foretelling the future, was already established by his blessing the warriors to whom he predicted the success or failure of their proposed raids. An Imenti elder described the divining aspect of the Mugwe's power in a more general way: ' This man (the Mugwe) was of the kind of diviners and he was cared for by God,' *muntu uju ari muthemba jwa kiruria ni ja kuuga ni akaragua ni Murungu.*

132 THE MUGWE, A FAILING PROPHET

The Imenti Mugwe was also described as having the power to go into a trance, when he would shout and behave like a madman. He could even hear things as if they were being told from the air. M. Mugwiria M. Kiria, another Imenti elder, recalled how a severe famine was foretold by the Mugwe of the Imenti, and how it came true; it was indeed a serious calamity and became known as Kiaramu.

The information on the Mugwe of the Chuka, Igembe and Tigania, does not offer any special evidence on this point. Among the Igembe, however, as we already know, there is a famous diviner, M. Lunyiru M. Ithiria, who is also called Mugwe. To study his functions and how he is regarded by his own people, the Igembe, may help to indicate more clearly the difference between the Mugwe proper and a diviner, *kiruria*.

M. Lunyiru states that the power of divining has always been in his family. His father, M. Ithiria, was a diviner, and diviners were his forefathers. It would seem, therefore, that divining is an hereditary profession for M. Lunyiru's family. But, at the same time, M. Lunyiru described how he was not nominated to inherit this power by his father, nor did he automatically succeed to the profession at his father's death or retirement. He experienced a personal call, long after his father's death, which came to him directly from God in a dream. Following this, came his 'investiture', also directly from God, this time in the form of a spell of madness. He ran amok and was subject to fits of violence. When this spell came to an end, it was accepted by everybody as genuine evidence of God's approval.

This story seems to indicate that divining comes as a personal call from God, and cannot, therefore, be regarded as an heritage. Some informants were sceptical about

THE POWER OF THE MUGWE

133

M. Lunyiru's story, and alleged that he had appointed himself to his profession as a diviner, and had been clever enough to produce signs to make his call appear supernatural.

If we compare the accession of M. Lunyiru with the accession of any of the Agwe proper, we notice that not only does the nomination of the Mugwe proper come to him primarily as a right of heritage, but that it is always a public affair. The selection of a candidate is made from among the family of the Mugwe, and his nomination is the right of the Mugwe proper and of the elders of his lineage who have a say as to the moral character of the candidate. The accession is always a solemn and public event both in the system of the Chuka, Imenti, and Tharaka, where it comes after the death of the old Mugwe, and in that of the Igembe-Tigania, where it occurs at the time of the blessing of a new age-class.

M. Lunyiru himself stressed another difference of his power from that of the Mugwe proper by stating that he has nothing to do with the age-classes. Blessing the age-classes is a specific power of the Mugwe proper, not only among the Igembe, but indeed among all the Meru sub-tribes. For this reason, therefore, the office of the Mugwe proper may be considered as a public office as opposed to the private character of the diviner.

The power of M. Lunyiru is especially invoked for blessing seeds, fields and harvests. He may also be asked to offer sacrifices of sheep and goats for the same reason. To assure the fertility of the fields he is to bless, he distributes portions of the sacrifice, which will be placed on trees or on posts in the fields. On all these occasions, which occur periodically during the year, he is visited by the Igembe women who go to him in a procession singing prayers and carrying offerings of every kind of food. Such

134 THE MUGWE, A FAILING PROPHET

prayers are in the form of an alternating litany, as follows:

1. On the way there:

Ngai ngwatia:	Ngai, help me:
Ni we Mugwe.	He is the Mugwe.
Mbura ngwatia:	Rain, help me:
Ni we Mugwe.	He is the Mugwe.
M. Lunyiru wetu:	M. Lunyiru of ours:
Ni we Mugwe.	He is the Mugwe.
Mbura ngwatia:	Rain, help me:
Ni we Mugwe.	He is the Mugwe.

2. At the residence of the Mugwe M. Lunyiru:

Ee, mwana mucii:	Ehe, son of the house;
teekia eiri.	hear our prayers.[1]
Mpande kinoria:	Increase our wealth:
Ee, mwana mucii.	Ehe, son of the house.
Ee, mwana mucii:	Ehe, son of the house:
Ee, mwana mucii.	Ehe, son of the house.

3. On the way back:

Ee, twana:	Ehe, we come back:
kwa Mugwe.	from the Mugwe.
M. Lunyiru:	M. Lunyiru:
ni we Mugwe.	He is the Mugwe.
Ee, Kilimara:	Ehe, Mount Kenya:
ni kia Mugwe.	It is of the Mugwe.
Ee, Nyambene:	Ehe, Mount Nyambene:
ni ya Mugwe.	It is of the Mugwe.

The visits and invocations of women to M. Lunyiru are in striking contrast to the normal prohibition on women making contact with the Mugwe proper, even when seeds or fields are to be blessed. In similar cases, even when there is a serious drought threatening the crops, the Mugwe is asked to bless the fields and the country but the request is

[1] Lit. 'remove the obstacles', i.e. the branches that surround and close the byre.

THE POWER OF THE MUGWE 135

always made by the elders. Indeed, the elders of the Igembe, commenting on the activity of M. Lunyiru and on his position in contrast to that of the Mugwe proper, said with some contempt: ' He is known only to women.' This statement also emphasizes the limitations of the diviner with regard to Meru social structure: being ' known to women ' means that he does not really fit into those structural institutions that are based on the elders and on their age-classes, as the Mugwe proper does.

It was not possible to establish for certain how M. Lunyiru came to be known also by the name of Mugwe. There are, of course, apparent similarities between his office and that of the Mugwe. He blesses, he wears similar insignia, such as a black staff and a dark brown mantle of goat-skins. With regard to the latter, it is significant that while I was not allowed to see the sacred mantle of the Mugwe proper of the Igembe at Antubocio (and the strongest objection came always from the elders who were present at my interviews: ' It is our secret,' they maintained) I experienced no difficulty with M. Lunyiru, nor did those present raise any objection to his readiness to comply with my requests. But though M. Lunyiru is called Mugwe, there is no mistake regarding his status with the Igembe elders. One of them, M. Imwae M. Mukena declared: ' The son of M. Ithiria is not regarded as the Mugwe; his work is similar to the work of the medicine-man, i.e. *kuraguranira*.' This is the attitude of the elders to him, which leaves no doubt that if M. Lunyiru is called Mugwe it is only an extension of the term, an undoubted mark of high regard for him and his work, but not because he shares in any way the power of the Ugwe.

As regards the activity of the Mugwe there seems to be sufficient evidence to state that he could also act as a

136   THE MUGWE, A FAILING PROPHET

diviner. Such an activity, however, goes with the power of
blessing which is peculiar to the Mugwe as the leader and
chief of his people. We can, therefore, say that while a
diviner, *kiruria*, is primarily and solely a diviner, and
therefore a private individual, the Mugwe is first and
foremost a public dignitary who, in carrying out his
responsibility for the well-being of his country and people,
may also act, but only incidentally and secondarily, as a
diviner.

8. PROPHET RATHER THAN PRIEST

Owing to the present state of decadence of Meru
institutions it was not possible to test the actual extension
of the Mugwe's authority in real life on any but a small
scale. This little confirmed the information of many
elders gathered from all the opposite corners of Meruland. Though the evidence is, thus, mainly verbal, it
leaves no doubt regarding the importance of the Mugwe
as one of the main pivots of the old Meru social structure.
How it fits into, and how it is related to, the other institutions of that structure, will be seen more clearly in the
next chapter.

In order to summarize the ideas regarding the power
of the Mugwe, we must first state that his power originates
from the Meru concept of the Divinity, as the Almighty
and the All-giver. The authority of the Mugwe is derived
from God, and the Mugwe represents God among his own
people. His actions, which are supposed to be always good,
are accepted and cited by the elders in support of their
belief. Secondly, the authority of the Mugwe is not for a
single individual but extends over the whole of his own
people, and he is supposed to look after the well-being
and the continuity of them all. The Mugwe is looked up
to as ' their father ', and his authority has the character

THE POWER OF THE MUGWE 137

of parental authority. It is in this sense, as representative of God and as their father, that the terms ‘leader and chief’, so frequently applied to the Mugwe, are to be understood. For the same reason, the power of the Mugwe is mainly described in terms of blessing. The Mugwe is there to bless.

Blessing the age-classes is described as the primary duty of the Mugwe. He blesses them from their inception at the initiation, and thus controls the setting up of the internal men’s organization, the mechanism by which authority is distributed and balanced among the various groups of his people, and, therefore, the first source of political authority. The formulæ that he uses in blessing show how conscious he is of this himself. He always refers to the country as *his* own country, to the people as *his* own people. Also, when he blesses a private person, his blessing and his interests are extended over the whole of his people. This universal character of the power and interests of the Mugwe is certainly a distinguishing mark of his office.

The authority of the Mugwe is also supported by sanctions and curses, expressed in imprecatory invocations complimentary to the first benevolent blessing. The sanctions and curses of the Mugwe are of a supernatural character: they work automatically and with certainty, even if they appear to be delayed. The fear of such sanctions adds tremendous weight and reality to the authority of the Mugwe.

The religious and moral character of the Mugwe’s authority is reflected in the attitude of the elders and of all the people towards him. It is evident from all the descriptions given and from my own personal observation that behaviour towards the Mugwe is dictated by a sense of admiration, respect, and awe. There is a *pietas*, a consciousness of duty, made up of loyalty and expectation,

138   THE MUGWE, A FAILING PROPHET

towards him as their parent. The presence of the Mugwe in the midst of his people is taken as a permanent guarantee of the continuity and prosperity of the country.

Nevertheless, the religious and moral character of the authority of the Mugwe is first and foremost reflected in the personality of the Mugwe himself. Since the time of his nomination as a candidate to the office, his character is the object of special attention and consideration, and his education is closely followed. At the time of his election, this is regarded in some ways as of even greater importance than the hereditary principle. When in office, his moral position is very unusual because, it is explained, the goodness of his life has to vouchsafe for the efficacy of all his blessings.

The man who becomes Mugwe is set aside or segregated, as it were, from the ordinary man on account of his office. He will do no work other than that of taking care of his country, of his people and of their well-being. In this sense it would not seem incorrect to speak of the Mugwe as a priest, and of the Mugwe institution as the tribal priesthood of the Meru. For the Mugwe is not only this. Even at present, when his power as leader has been entirely superseded by the administrative chiefs, it is this status of his, as leader and chief, that was most stressed by my informants. Moreover, if he is regarded only as a priest, the power of offering sacrifices to God should be his exclusive prerogative. This, however, is not so. He may sometimes advise on the right time to offer a sacrifice, and may also offer sacrifices in his own capacity, but the right of offering remains the general privilege of the *ntindiri* elders. These elders, as is known, have reached a stage when they are supposed to be unable to commit sin; they have also attained the highest social status and are regarded as the highest living representatives of parental

THE POWER OF THE MUGWE 139

authority; every such elder is thought, therefore, to be *persona grata* with God: hence their privilege of offering sacrifices.

But the Mugwe is as holy as any of the *ntindiri* elders. Indeed, he is higher than they are, because his parental authority, as the father of all his people, is wider and more embracing than theirs; also, his ' holiness ' is greater because he is the Mugwe, and we have seen how he was matched to a *ntindiri* old woman to make sure of his absolute holiness. He can, then, on his own initiative offer sacrifices to God; but this does not in any way whatsoever limit the rights of the *ntindiri* elders.

Moreover, every other elder, if he is the head of a lineage, can perform sacrifices and other religious rites for his own lineage. This happens in time of crisis, such as death, marriage, or initiation of members.

Political matters, on the other hand, were also the subject of the assemblies or councils of the elders. In this respect the Mugwe is the leader and chief not only because he controls the setting up of the age-groups, but also because he has power, as we shall see, to lead the elders' assemblies, and could intervene in his personal capacity on matters of general concern. All the evidence points to the political extension of the Mugwe's authority. It is thus that the continued existence of his people and the prosperity of his country are guaranteed by the presence of the Mugwe in their midst.

The peculiar character of the Mugwe is already noticeable in the deeds of the first Mugwe. Some accounts of those deeds have been mentioned already in a previous section. It seems relevant to record here a most singular narration dictated by M. Muga of Chokarige about the first Mugwe of the Tharaka:

Mugwe (a name that is given as the personal name of the

140 THE MUGWE, A FAILING PROPHET

first Mugwe) was the leader of the Tharaka who left Mbwa. By stroking the water with his staff, he let them cross the water with dry feet. When they arrived at their present land, Mugwe divided them up into clans; he set the boundaries of the land on which they were to live and cultivate. He instituted the age-groups in order to co-ordinate the activity of them all. For training the young initiates and exploiting their strength he established the *gaaru*, the house in which they were to live by themselves and be ready to defend their country from the attacks of the enemies. He gave them the commandments, as follows: 1. Thou shalt not steal; 2. thou shalt not try to take anything by force; 3. thou shalt not kill (to kill is very bad); 4. thou shalt not try to take another man's wife; 5. everybody must keep his own things. He had power to enforce sanctions on trespassers. He could cause the death of those who refused to respect and obey him.

The above description shows the Mugwe in a function very different from that of a simple priest. He is really a leader, a reformer, and a law-maker. In addition, we have already noted that among the successors of the first Mugwe, it is the general well-being of their people rather than of the individual that distinguishes their office. We saw how he controls the initiation and formation of new age-classes, and how no military exploits could take place without his previous consent.

All these facts make it more correct, I think, to regard the Mugwe as a prophet, i.e. a leader with both religious and political powers, rather than as a priest.

Chapter Six

THE POSITION OF THE MUGWE IN THE SOCIAL STRUCTURE

I. IN THE SUB-TRIBE

The division of the Meru into sub-tribes and the partition of land among them was due, according to the elders, to the necessity of finding good farming land for all of them and to the need for avoiding, as far as possible, feuds and internecine quarrels. Since their division each sub-tribe has developed more or less independently to become, in fact, a self-contained social and political unit. Their structure, their age-organization, their ceremonies and rituals are all very similar, though local differences may be stressed, even at the present day, to throw into relief the individuality of each sub-tribe as such. Conversely, and at the same time, similarities may be emphasized to show that the Meru are one related tribe.

This situation is clearly reflected in the institution of the Mugwe. *Agwe ni babainge na Ugwe ni bumwe, indi o muntu na nthiguru yawe,* ' the Agwe are many and the Ugwe is one, but every man (Mugwe) has his own territory '. The power of the Ugwe is not something that differs from one place to another or from one man to another, but the Mugwe is different. There is not one single Mugwe for all the Meru, but many Agwe, each with his own area and his own people. These areas coincide with the territory of the Meru sub-tribes, except for the Mwimbi group. This group, as noted above, does not recognize the Mugwe proper, but we have seen in this evidence for considering the association of the Mwimbi to the other Meru to be a recent event, as asserted by the elders of other sub-tribes.

142   THE MUGWE, A FAILING PROPHET

The problem now is to single out the significance of the Mugwe in the structure of the sub-tribe. Tradition, it is seen, would have the present plurality of the Agwe derived from a natural genealogical fission from a single family. Such a tradition, for all its value, may be taken as another piece of evidence to show the fundamental unity of the Ugwe as a single power, but for the actual structure of the sub-tribe it is of no consequence. It is the individual Mugwe and his actual family who matter for a single sub-tribe. All the analysis already made indicates how intimately the Mugwe is connected with the organization and activity of his people. Indeed, he is looked upon as the focal point of their structure. It is true that the effectiveness of his influence depends a great deal on the personality and the character of the actual Mugwe himself. We shall see in the next chapter how much bearing this has on the modern development of the institution. There is no doubt, however, that, independently of the actual person, the presence of the Mugwe constitutes a strong factor of union and social cohesion. In this sense, again, he is ' the leader and the chief '. This is especially true for the times before European administration. The elders are consistent in saying that at that time there was no other chief but the Mugwe. The term they use, *munene*, may at present also be applied to chiefs appointed by the Administration, and may therefore be misleading. It is known that Meru, in the past, did not have chiefs in the sense we commonly use this word, viz. men with executive authority. Nor was the Mugwe such a chief. *Munene* is the man who has the power, *unene* is that power. For this reason, the term *cibu* tends now to replace the word *munene*, as describing better the new office of a modern chief. The Mugwe, as the man who had the power of the Ugwe, was *munene*. The Ugwe is a singular power, as we

THE POSITION OF THE MUGWE 143

have seen. It extends over all the people, it can be held only by inheritance, and by certain individuals. Thus, the Mugwe is the only man with this power, and the only one whose authority extends over all the people. In this special sense only, he can be described as a chief or as a king. In his own sub-tribe there is no limitation to the authority of the Mugwe: *Mugwe aari ja munene wa antu bonthe ba nthiguru cionthe, ti ati ni Kirirwa gunka, ni nthiguru o iriku kana iriku* 'the Mugwe the chief of all the men of all territories, not only of Kirirwa but of every territory'. This statement by an Imenti elder shows clearly the universality of the power of the Imenti Mugwe. Territories, in this context, refer to the other areas of the Imenti. A similar statement was made by M. Kiganka of the Chuka: *Ugwe bubu bwakwa ni bwa nthiguru yonthe ya Chuka, ti bwa kinya mwiriga kana bwakwa ningwa*, 'this Ugwe of mine is for the whole country of Chuka, and not for my clan or for myself alone'.

The authority and the presence of the Mugwe were regarded as a guarantee of prosperity. Even at the present time the elders look upon him as the safeguard for all that is good and still remains of the old system: 'If there were no Mugwe the country would not prosper as before.' His insignia, especially the *kiragu* and the sacred honey, are considered to be the tribal symbols, of which he is the custodian. Somehow these symbols and insignia are a public concern, as is the Mugwe as such. Indeed 'he must not be let to suffer'. All his people volunteered to work for him, building his house, erecting his fences, cultivating his fields and even today, as I was told among the Tigania, contributing towards his personal tax. Indeed, fees to the Mugwe were paid everywhere among the Meru: in sheep, goats, honey and honey-beer, and other kinds ot food. These fees were not in the nature of obligatory

144 THE MUGWE, A FAILING PROPHET

tithes, but were free contributions. *Ni wendi bwao*, 'it is all due to their goodness', stated M. Mugambi, the Mugwe of the Igembe, pointing to the houses in his homestead built by his people. In the mind of the elders the sub-tribe (the country, the people) will persist as long as the Mugwe is there; it will prosper if the Mugwe prospers; it will perish if the Mugwe fails. It is thus possible to see a sort of identity between the Mugwe and the sub-tribe for which and among which he stands.

Against this form of identity and the asserted universality of the authority of the Mugwe seem to stand the dual divisions of the inner organization of the Meru sub-tribes. Among the Tharaka the phenomenon appears to be most relevant. The Tharaka of Urio were not expected to visit the Mugwe, while those of Umotho were entirely dependent on him; he was described as belonging to them. The distinction was somehow felt in social intercourse, and the Umotho Tharaka looked down on those of Urio. Such a limitation of the power of the Mugwe was, however, only apparent. In fact and in practice his authority extended to all the Tharaka without distinction: *indi ni untu bwa kiao kiawe ni atumaga ntharimi na antu bangi baria bejagira cio*, 'but for his mercy he sends (them) blessings through those others who come for being blessed'. And not only did the Mugwe send his blessing to those of Urio, but he summoned them to war or to any other gathering by sending messengers with his staff as a seal of his authority. It is with reference to this power to summon all the Tharaka that one elder described him as the focal point for them all: 'When there was a gathering, all the Tharaka came to see him. Also those from Thagicu came, even when the Tana was flooded, crossing the river by rafts made from palm-trees (*miari*). They all wanted to see their chief, the Mugwe.' It seems, therefore, correct to

THE POSITION OF THE MUGWE 145

regard the Mugwe as the cohesive factor by which all the separating effects of the dual divisions were overcome.

On the other hand, another phenomenon should be noted. The existence of two dignitaries among the Tigania, the Mugwe and the Mukiama, with the same power for each of the dual divisions of the Tigania, is also indicative of the centralizing power of their office. The dual divisions of the Tigania had reached a stage of virtual independence which, had it not been checked by modern administration, would very probably have led to the formation of two new sub-tribes. The two divisions still consider themselves Tigania, but the process of separation had gone a long way, as is shown by the performance of the age-rituals, the initiation and the *ntuiko*, held independently of one another. The Mukiama of the Athwana-Tigania is described and regarded, to all effects, as a Mugwe proper and the Athwana centre around him in the same way as the Igoki-Tigania centre around the Mugwe. It is probable that the Mukiama reached his present position from an earlier state of subordination to the Mugwe proper.

A very similar problem arises with regard to the position and function of the Assistant Agwe. A number of these subordinate functionaries have been recorded among the Chuka. They are described as having the rôle of local representatives of the Mugwe to whom they were expected to lead their people. All the territorial sections of the Chuka had one such functionary. When I made enquiries about the possibility of the Assistant Agwe rebelling against the Mugwe, the hypothesis was dismissed as something unthinkable. The development of the Mukiama among the Tigania, however, offers evidence that such a thing might be possible. The position of the Assistant

146   THE MUGWE, A FAILING PROPHET

Mugwe offers him the possibility of fostering the unity of his local section in opposition to the sub-tribe, thereby setting up a new sub-tribe.

A situation similar to that of the Assistant Agwe exists with regard to the Mugwe-diviner. He also is called by the honorific name of Mugwe. Among the Igembe the Mugwe-diviner is sometimes confused with the Mugwe proper by the new generations, not so well acquainted with matters concerning the Mugwe. It is also very significant that among the Mwimbi group the diviner was called by the same honorific name, Mugwe, somehow filling the rôle of a Mugwe proper which they did not possess. Evidently, in the hands of a shrewd man, and given proper circumstances, the position of the Mugwe-diviner could be so enhanced as to make it a power similar to that of the actual Mugwe. I am of the opinion that the asserted existence of a Mugwe proper among the Igoji by some of the elders, is due to the development of this situation.

It is not possible to establish with certainty the historical developments that led to the establishment of the authority of the Mugwe or of the Mukiama. But whatever those developments were, it seems certain that when a man reaches the status of Mugwe, he becomes a stabilizing factor around which the structure of his sub-tribe or section gravitates. There is no question of an ambivalence of force with the Mugwe proper, as if he were the cause of new sections breaking away and at the same time the unifying factor of every section. The Mugwe, as such, is a guarantee of cohesion and a safeguard against disintegration. The unifying relationship of the Mugwe to every member of a sub-tribe can be summarized by the following saying by an Imenti elder: ' For the Mugwe,' he said, ' there cannot be a son of the breast and a son of the

THE POSITION OF THE MUGWE 147

back, but all are the same,' *gutiri wa nda na wa mugongo*.

2. IN THE CLAN, LINEAGE, AND FAMILY

Though the authority of the Mugwe extends over the whole of his sub-tribe and he refers to them as ' my people ' and ' my country ', the family of the Mugwe and his lineage (though not so much his clan, as distinct from his lineage), are normally described as ' the people of the Mugwe '. The position is self-evident. The Mugwe is *ex officio*, as it were, the head and the leader of his own lineage. There is no *mugambi* who can be above him in his clan. As the leader of his lineage, the Mugwe is assisted by the elders of the lineage itself, who form the inner council of the lineage, the same as any other lineage or clan. I witnessed the functioning of this council among the Tharaka, the Chuka and the Igembe. There was nothing formal about it, but it was clear that the Mugwe was the dominant figure. We shall analyse the subject further below when we discuss the relationship of the Mugwe with the elders.

Within his own family, *mucii*, the Mugwe is merely the father. The system of succession to the Ugwe, by which the right of primogeniture is not so strictly followed, makes the position of the Mugwe's homestead no different from that of any other homestead of his lineage. Indeed, his authority with regard to his own family is private, and it is not altered or enlarged by his official status. Even if his son has already been nominated as the successor to the Ugwe, the Mugwe would act no differently from any other elder of his lineage who might become the genitor of the candidate for the honour of Mugwe. This confirms the ' public ' character of the Mugwe's authority and office which has been stressed repeatedly before. The position of the Mugwe in relation to his lineage and his family is of a

148 THE MUGWE, A FAILING PROPHET

different kind from that by which he is connected to the whole of his people: the former is a private and natural relationship, the latter a public and official one.

The position of the lineage of the Mugwe with relation to other clans is a different problem.

Each clan may be differentiated in a special way— because of its numbers, wealth, and the bravery of its members; of magical powers attributed to the clan itself; or because of the general moral character of its members. The evaluation of clans by outsiders may differ, of course, according to places and individuals, and also according to the inner lineages of the same clan. In one part of Tharaka for instance, Kanjugu, Kamurige and Gankena clans were described as the most powerful because of their large numbers. In another part of Tharaka, Mbura and Utanga clans were regarded as the bravest in fighting. Among the Tigania, Antubaita, the sons of the mythological Gaita, are said to be distinguished for their intelligence and powers of leadership.

But, the clan of the Mugwe is the greatest of them all. ' Even if there were only ten people in that clan,' stated an elder, ' it would still be the greatest of them all.' It is the presence of the Mugwe that makes his clan great, though it must be added that the clan does not constitute any form of aristocracy. Special powers are attributed to its members, but it appears that sometimes there is confusion between the powers of the Mugwe as such and those of his clan. Generally it is said that among all the sub-tribes the clan of the Mugwe has power over the rain, because the rain-making rituals of the elders of that clan are considered to be most powerful.

The clan of the Tharaka Mugwe, Kithuri, is thought to know specially powerful curses, for which reason it was praised by an elder as advantageous to the order of the

THE POSITION OF THE MUGWE 149

country: ' We are afraid of Kithuri people,' he said, ' so, whenever we catch any man who does not behave properly we take him to the elders of that clan so that they may curse him.' Misbehaviour, generally, refers to stealing, but it is not clear in this context whether the elders referred to were the elders of Kithuri clan as such, or the Mugwe assisted by the elders of this clan.

Also among the Tharaka I found that a clear distinction is made between the Mugwe and the people of his clan. While the Mugwe is above criticism, because ' he is good ', members of his clan are not necessarily as good, and may be severely criticized. ' Kithuri people,' remarked a Tharaka elder, ' are so called because they are mean and bad. They possess powers that they use to their own advantage. In general, they are selfish, egoistical, and make few friends. If anyone steals from them there is no restitution: he must die. If a young man breaks his friendship with a girl from that clan there is no alternative for him: he must die. If you take food from that clan they will speak after you, saying that yours is a very big stomach, and that is a curse that will make you unable to take more food in the future.' The elder who spoke thus was a friend of mine; I knew him as a reliable elder, and he surprised me with his strong words. There was no doubt that he was speaking with resentment. But, as if he had grown afraid of the consequences of what he had been saying, he asked that I should keep this interview to myself. Then, by way of conclusion, he added: ' But the Mugwe is good.' The distinction between the Mugwe and his clan is significant. It indicates that the official status of the Mugwe is not to be confused with his clan membership and allegiance.

We have quoted above only evidence from the Tharaka, but the situation is similar among the other sub-tribes.

150 THE MUGWE, A FAILING PROPHET

Among the Imenti, even at present, the Umu clan is greatly revered and feared on account of the *kiragu*, the insignia of the Mugwe's power.[1]

While fees were paid to the Mugwe, who should not be allowed to suffer loss, it was his family that benefited from the advantages of communal co-operation. Even when a fine, for murder or for adultery, has been imposed on the Mugwe's clan, according to common law, not only must the whole of this clan pay but, being the clan of the Mugwe, contributions are demanded and offered from other clans also.

Although the family and lineage of the Mugwe enjoy many practical advantages, the important point to note is that the clan of the Mugwe does not, as such, enjoy any special consideration in the total structure of the sub-tribe. Special consideration is entirely and solely reserved for the person of the Mugwe.

3. THE MUGWE AND THE ELDERS

Elderhood is a basic structural principle of the social and political organization of the Meru. The elders control all forms of social and political activities and are the real masters of the country. Such control is exercised first in the inner councils of the elders of the clan, secondly in the larger assemblies of all the elders, and finally in the association and inner councils of the *njuri*.

The relationship of the Mugwe to the elders must be viewed in the light of the supremacy of this principle and of the peculiar status of the Mugwe himself. Two considerations are to be made with regard to the Mugwe. He

[1] The headman, under whose authority Kirirwa, the old place of the Mugwe of the Imenti, falls had ordered all women of his area to carry some *macoro*, dry banana-leaves for thatching, to Kaongo Market and keep them separate for each place: Kaongo one heap, Kariene one heap, Kirirwa, etc. While he used all the other leaves, he never touched the leaves from Kirirwa for fear any evil should befall him and his family.

THE POSITION OF THE MUGWE 151

is, first, a sacred person with a public official status, unique in character, the holder of the sacred symbols of the country, and the guarantor of the prosperity and continuity of his people. As such, there is no one who can be above him. Though the elders are the fathers, it is only the Mugwe who can be called the father of the people or of the country. Indeed, he is the great parent, *babu u munene*. On the other hand, he can also be regarded, in his status as an ordinary man, as being himself an elder. It follows that the Mugwe can, and in fact does, assume two different positions among and with regard to the elders: one, which is official, as the Mugwe; the other, which is private, as an elder among elders.

The elders may be connected with the Mugwe through their councils, by which they are called to assist him in his office. But we need to distinguish two different situations. One is that of the elders of all clans and age-classes, who in their capacity as elders may sit on the councils and thereby contribute to the discussion of affairs. The other is that of the elders of the Mugwe's lineage who, for this very reason, have special interests in all things of the Ugwe, and, besides forming an inner council, always at hand when the Mugwe needs their assistance, tend to form a compact group when matters are discussed.

The function of these councils of elders with relation to the Mugwe was described as follows by M. Mugambi M. Ikiara, an elder of the Imenti: ' The elders go to assist him (the Mugwe) because they say that he is like their *Kajene* (queen of the bees) whom they have to protect from the *muthwa* (termites).'

Where the *njuri* association is still effective, as among the Igembe, the Mugwe is eagerly co-opted as a member. Among the other sub-tribes affiliation to the *njuri* is not

152   THE MUGWE, A FAILING PROPHET

thought to be relevant. In any case, all the elders are quite definite in stating that the Mugwe is also above the *njuri*: none can be above him. The association of the *njuri* as such, therefore, has no special relation to the Mugwe in his official capacity. He can sit among the *njuri* as one of them, but I failed to discover any connecting link between the two institutions.

When the Mugwe is present at meetings of the elders, his influence is soon felt, as I have myself experienced. At Chera Village among the Chuka my first interview with M. Kiganka, the Mugwe, took place in the presence of the full council of village elders, where the past of the Chuka and their present situation were discussed; it was my introduction to those who were to become my good friends. At first conversation was general; then the most senior, M. Rendire M. Anduju, took the lead, answering all my questions with intelligence and shrewdness. At one point M. Kiganka, who had hitherto remained silent among the crowd, indicated that he would join in the conversation. The senior elder broke off what he was saying and retired quietly among the other elders. M. Kiganka continued with animation. The others did not join in, except when expressly asked to do so by M. Kiganka himself.

Some months after this first meeting, M. Kiganka asked for my assistance in contacting the Mugwe of Igembe. I went to Chera and the same elders were present. When I expressed my pleasure in being offered an opportunity to assist him, M. Kiganka did not reply directly but turned to the elders as if expecting their opinion. They retired to a secluded spot and left us alone, M. Kiganka, my assistant, and myself, to await their decision. It came after some time and was favourable.

M. Mugambi, the Mugwe of the Igembe, behaved in a

THE POSITION OF THE MUGWE 153

similar way when I passed on to him the message from M. Kiganka. He asked for more time in order that he might consult with his elders.

These two instances illustrate well the relationship of the Mugwe to the elders. Both constitute two fundamental institutions of the social and political structure of the Meru, and both are intimately connected. While the Mugwe is regarded as the symbol of tribal unity and continuity, the elders do in fact constitute the governing body representing the living people. The Mugwe stands higher than the elders, for he represents in his official status the unity of all his people beyond and above any limit of time ('the Mugwe cannot die'); the elders make up the actual governing council which must be consulted for their views and opinions on current affairs. The position of the Mugwe among the elders is not simply that of a *primus inter pares*. He is definitely above them all, though, at first, and to a superficial observer, he may simply appear as a greater *mugambi* among his equals.

An episode from my first experience of the Tharaka may supply further evidence of the great regard that the elders have for the Mugwe. It occurred during my first interview with M. Ruanda, the Mugwe of the Tharaka. Two very old men, M. Muga and Nkeya, were also present. M. Muga has a forceful personality, is very intelligent, and was formerly a great *mugambi;* now he is blind. Nkeya is the old circumciser. Conversation had proceeded smoothly and satisfactorily, M. Muga providing all the answers. Then I managed to turn directly to M. Ruanda, whom I was anxious to interview personally. Apparently M. Muga resented my direct questioning of M. Ruanda. At one point, I had just put a further question asking for more information on Mutuampea, M. Ruanda's great-grandfather, when suddenly M.

Muga stood up in front of me saying: 'Why do you ask all these questions?' and for a while looked blindly ahead with an expression of fixed indignation. There was a smile of satisfaction on M. Ruanda's face. Nkeya kept looking at me as if expecting an answer. I apologized and said that, being a newcomer to their country, I still did not know their customs properly. I had failed to see anything wrong in my questioning, but I should be only too grateful to be taught the correct way. The air was cleared. M. Muga rejoined that he knew I was their friend; they would still consider me as such, but the Mugwe was their chief and leader. The incident closed at that. I and my work did not suffer because of it. On the contrary, it served to excite my curiosity about the peculiar status of the Mugwe.

The matters in which the Mugwe is assisted by the elders, or which he discusses with them, are the following: deciding the time for holding the *ntuiko* and for blessing the age-classes; matters regarding the Ugwe and concerning the whole country, such as contacting the Mugwe of another sub-tribe in order to beg his help in time of special trouble; the conduct and the training of the initiates during the time in the *gaaru*; deciding a suitable time for a raid; and changes in the traditional way of life.

The legislative and judicial authority of the Mugwe is not stressed, because such activities are controlled by the councils of the elders on which the Mugwe sits, generally in his private capacity as an elder. In any case, matters of law and justice are of such a nature as to demand long discussions and interpretations; therefore the authority of the Mugwe is not required except for sanctioning the final decisions, especially if they entail capital punishment.

In all other small everyday matters the elders proceed

THE POSITION OF THE MUGWE 155

without any special assistance from the Mugwe. Indeed the external machinery of tribal government and of social life would appear to work satisfactorily even without the Mugwe. That it does not do so, at least in the minds of the Meru, is confirmed by the unanimous opinion of all the elders that the country's general condition is satisfactory only if the authority of the Mugwe is efficient; things go wrong, as during the Mau Mau rebellion, if the Mugwe is no longer respected and his authority disregarded.

4. THE MUGWE AND THE WARRIORS

The relationship of the Mugwe and the warriors or young initiates, *nthaka*, is of a very different nature: there is no question of an equal status between them. The function of the Mugwe as leader and chief extends to the initiates in a very special way; but his relationship to them is distinguished from all other such by its master-pupil aspect, the Mugwe being the tutor, as it were, of the young initiates. Initiates, as we know, are soon organized into inner councils at which they settle their own problems. The Mugwe does not have a seat on these councils, but he must be consulted on all important matters and his word is final.

Young initiates were expected to ' know ' the Mugwe. ' Knowing ' the Mugwe, which is the same thing as being ' blessed ' by him, can be considered as another essential part of the long initiation process of the Meru. Uninitiated boys were kept from any contact with the Mugwe. It was generally at the *ntuiko* festival that the ' knowing-blessing ' took place, but the initiates were free to organize private visits to the Mugwe, especially if they were contemplating some raid. While they were on their way to him, they used to sing, exalting their *gaaru* and their arms:

156   THE MUGWE, A FAILING PROPHET

Uu, gaaru, uu, ruthiu. Uu (our), unit, uu (our), booty.
Uu, gaaru, uu, ruthiu. Uu (our), unit, uu (our), booty.

They were not allowed to set foot beyond the fence of the Mugwe's house and should not approach holding their spears.

The initiates of the Mugwe's own lineage, of course, stood in a special relationship to him. It was he who handed them the spear, the sword, the fighting-stick (*matumo, mpiu, ma rung'u*), at a ceremony which, for the other initiates, was performed by their own fathers.

While the initiates were in the *gaaru* the Mugwe used to visit and bless them. This was part of the basic ' knowing-blessing ' relationship, but it was at these visits particularly that the master-pupil aspect became apparent, an aspect that accords well with his description as the father of the people and the guarantor of their continuity. If an initiate should disgrace himself with an uninitiated girl, the sanction of the Mugwe was required, and he would either confirm the sentence of the elders' council, even if it were capital, or summon the guilty boy to the *gaaru* and direct his companions to avenge their shame by lashing and beating the culprit.

Dependence of the initiates on the Mugwe was complete, especially with regard to military activity. Even after their inner council of war had decided on a raid, this could not take place unless the Mugwe had been previously informed and had given his blessing. In addition, if, as could happen especially in remote parts, a *mugaa* had been consulted, the Mugwe still had to be informed and his blessing obtained. It was a condition for the success of the venture.[1]

[1] The following information by Rev. Father Cavicchi is pertinent: ' While I was inspecting the School at Imenti Mission (1946), I was present

THE POSITION OF THE MUGWE 157

Loyalty to the Mugwe was also expressed after a successful raid, when the victors were expected to pay a visit of thankfulness and to offer him a large portion of the spoils.

Because his blessing and assistance were required before and after any raid, the Mugwe could exercise real control over the activity of warriors and initiates. Indeed, this is still regarded by many of the elders as the best method of keeping order and of fostering the well-being of the country. By his control over the formation and activity of the age-set system, the Mugwe could direct and use the executive power.

Speaking of the accession of a new Mugwe we distinguished two systems: one, of the Igembe and Tigania, marked by a more personal relationship between the new Mugwe and the age-class that he blesses at the *ntuiko;* the other, of the Tharaka, Chuka and Imenti, where a more universal relationship extended over all the age-classes. It is among the latter, as one would expect, that this universality is more stressed. ' The Mugwe,' stated one Tharaka elder, ' is not of a special *nthuki*, or age-class, nor of a special clan: he is of all his country, for he does not divide his sons from the others.' Which means, that though the Mugwe may be specially connected with an age-class that ' he visited and blessed ', he nevertheless aims at making every age-class a functioning unit in the larger structure of the sub-tribe.

5. THE THEORETICAL SIGNIFICANCE AND POSITION OF THE MUGWE IN THE SOCIAL STRUCTURE

In the light of the foregoing descriptions and analysis

at a lesson on tribal government by Teacher Isidoro M. Muthamia of Igane, to Standard IV. Speaking about how war was organized by the Meru, he explained that first the matter was discussed by the initiates in their council; then the *mugaa* was consulted. After that, all final decision rested with the Mugwe who is for the Meru what the Kabaka is for the Baganda and the King for the British. Only a few *njuri* knew about him.'

158 THE MUGWE, A FAILING PROPHET

we can now assess in a more general way the position of the Mugwe in the structure of the Meru sub-tribes and indicate the main theoretical principles underlying this position.

The mythological accounts of the origin of the Mugwe make him a kind of living link between the present and past generations. He is supposed to be the descendant of the first leader of the Meru, of the first Mugwe. From this point of view already the Mugwe must be regarded as the guarantee of the continuity and prosperity of the Meru.

The descent of the living Mugwe from the first Mugwe is a condition of office and introduces the principle of hereditary succession in the structure of the Meru. Among the Meru there is no other institution of general importance, apart from kinship, based on this principle. Authority and political power are not inherited; they can be attained, after initiation, by any of the men, and in this respect their status, primarily defined by initiation, is equal and can be modified only by personal achievements. The power of the Ugwe, by contrast, is inherited, and by the members of a single lineage only. At the same time it is not something equally shared by all members, but something inherited in its totality by the elected candidate who becomes a public person through it. In one sense, therefore, the Ugwe is the personal power of the Mugwe that ' nobody can take away from him ', which, nevertheless, must not be exploited to his personal advantage, but must be used for the benefit of the whole country.

High moral character is essential for the Mugwe; and both his private and public life must conform to this high standard. In his relationship with his people, the Mugwe must not be partial: he is the father of them all. Though there are social differentiations: ' We are all the same, we

THE POSITION OF THE MUGWE 159

all came together, and because we came out all together, there cannot be the son of the breast and the son of the back,' *gutiri wa nda na wa mugongo*. The relationship of the Mugwe to his people as a whole is so intimate that it amounts to a kind of identification.

The unity to which we refer is naturally that of the sub-tribe. Every Mugwe is the head of his own sub-tribe. The differentiation and independence that marked the Meru sub-tribes was also reflected in the distribution and differentiation of the Agwe. Every Mugwe stands for himself and for his own people and none is, or can be, recognized as the head of all the Agwe. The point is even more surprising and noteworthy, because it is strongly asserted and mythologically supported that all the Agwe, whatever their present lineage or the denomination of their own clans, are descendants of a single original family.

The unique quality of the Mugwe's power is emphasized also by its religious character. Representing all his people as their father, he represents them to God. He prays to God for ' this people of mine '. Not only is he regarded as a man of God, but, in a manner of speaking, he is identified with God. Indeed, no other man could be compared to the Mugwe.

The religious aspect of the power of the Mugwe shows the religious character of his office, and confirms the universality of his power, which covers all the fundamental aspects of public activities and relations.

It must be stressed, however, that the Mugwe is not a minister of any particular cult, not of the High God nor of the ancestors. He is much more than this. All the elders, inasmuch as they perform cult rituals, are, so to speak, ministers of cults; a quality that is derived from their status as heads of family or lineage, and is specially enhanced when they reach the stage and status of *ntindiri*

160 THE MUGWE, A FAILING PROPHET

elders. The Mugwe can also serve in this capacity. But by his official status he represents God and is the Father of all.

The Mugwe is the custodian of the tribal symbols which are, to some extent, identified with the insignia of his power and office. The value of these symbols lies in their alleged derivation from the very origin of the sub-tribe or indeed, of all the Meru. Their presence is a guarantee of the country's continuity of which the Mugwe, because he is their custodian, is regarded as the guarantor.

The intimate connection of the Mugwe with the age-class system is also typical and a basic function of his office. Among the Igembe and the Tigania this is more in evidence because it is of a more prominent kind, but there is a similar relationship among the other sub-tribes. By the age-class system all the men are recruited, as it were, in order to share in the machinery of tribal government. The office of the Mugwe is quite distinct from the inner organization that goes to make up that machinery. In fact his office is necessary to this organization, and it is part of its function to assist in building it up and making it work. The Mugwe's control over this system, thanks to his power of blessing, re-emphasizes again his position as guarantor of the orderly continuity of his people. The essential work of the Mugwe is, indeed, to bless—to bless the country as a whole; to bless ' his sons ' in their social growth and exploits and to bless the individuals when their miserable condition can become a menace to the stability or continuity of the country.

The Mugwe is not merely a practitioner who has acquired an art and can be consulted for trivial private cases. His office is primarily for the general welfare. It is from God, fundamentally, that he derives his authority. The election that takes place at his accession has this aim:

THE POSITION OF THE MUGWE 161

to single him out from among his brothers as the right man for the job.

The authority of the Mugwe is, therefore, basically religious, but the control he can exert on the government machinery puts into his hands a potential source of political power. A strong man with ambition and shrewdness could certainly exploit it.

In his own family the Mugwe appears as an ordinary man. He does not surround himself with grandeur; there is no overt indication of his peculiar and exalted position. He is certainly no king; he is without court and without protocol.

With regard to his people also, his authority is fundamentally a parental authority. He does not reign or govern, but advises, blesses, and sanctions. He is a leader rather than a ruler, a prophet rather than a priest.

The structural importance of the Mugwe is emphasized by the attitude of the elders. All of them consistently recognize the Ugwe as a basic institution of the Meru sub-tribes and the Mugwe, its unique officer, as absolutely necessary. This recognition was expressed in a set of social rules and ritual and political ties peculiar to the Mugwe that still hold good in the evaluation of the elders. The situation is now rapidly changing with the new generations, but the elders greatly deplore the passing of such an important institution as that of the Mugwe.

6. SOME COMPARATIVE FIGURES

Before we proceed to describe the present situation of the Mugwe, I propose to analyse the structural significance of two other dignitaries, the Laibon of the Masai and the Hayu or Abba Boku of the Galla Boran, who have some obvious similarities with the Mugwe of the Meru.

The aim of this comparison is to show that the Mugwe

162 THE MUGWE, A FAILING PROPHET

is not an isolated figure on the anthropological map of East Africa; to underline the similarities and dissimilarities in structure and function between these other dignitaries and the Mugwe; and to assist in formulating a clearer statement of the problem of the cultural relations of the three peoples concerned, a problem which is not only far from being solved, but which still awaits wider and more thorough investigation of all the aspects involved. The Masai were, in the past, close neighbours of the Meru, inhabiting, as they did, the plains of Rumuruti and Nanyuki up to the Upper Imenti Forest. The Galla Boran, as has been already noted, inhabit all the plains north of the Meru with whom, even nowadays, they still practise some trade-exchange.

(a) *The Laibon of the Masai*

H. A. Fosbrooke[1] is still our best authority on the Masai Laibon, of which he distinguishes three types: (i) the independent practitioner, who is consulted by individual patients and who cures sickness and barrenness and ensures fidelity in wives: (ii) the independent practitioner of higher reputation, who is consulted by several districts and provides charms for the whole group to grant them success in war, rain for their grass, and fertility for their wives and cattle: (iii) a practitioner who, besides ' retaining the duties of the two previous, performs ceremonies and provides charms for a whole tribe '. In particular his duties to the whole tribe are as follows: (a) to sanction all raids and war and provide protective medicines for the warriors; (b) to authorize the ceremonies connected with the age-class system; (c) to guarantee the general well-being and fertility of his people; (d) to make rain.

It is this third type of practitioner who is regarded as the chief medicine man of the Masai sub-tribe. Fos-

[1] Fosbrooke, 1948, pp. 15-19. (See Bibliography.)

THE POSITION OF THE MUGWE 163

brooke remarks that it does not seem correct to assume that 'all the Masai acknowledged one Laibon'. He quotes the example of Mbatian who 'had a fellow practitioner, if not a rival, in his brother Mako'. One could also mention the sons of Mbatian, Sendeyo and Lenana, who were rivals until Lenana prevailed and was acknowledged by the Administration as 'Paramount Chief of all the Masai'. Besides, continues Fosbrooke, 'other rival sub-tribes, Uashingishu, Kwavi, etc., had their own medicine men.'

The chief Laibon must always be a member of the Engidong clan. The office is only broadly hereditary. There are 'no definite rules of succession, the choice resting on the general consent of the tribe', though a man trained and nominated by the previous Laibon would normally be chosen. This nomination, however, could also be overlooked, if there were a more powerful Laibon, and certainly if the nominee were found guilty of having killed the previous Laibon in order to take over his office ('for the death of a Laibon is as a matter of course attributed to witchcraft by a fellow Engidong, and the first step in choosing a new Laibon is to ascertain who killed the old ').

The three categories cited by Fosbrooke for the purpose of defining the position of the chief Laibon, do not constitute, as such, three special structural institutions. They are, in fact, three different stages of a career, the highest of which can be attained by any member of the Engidong clan, provided that he has the necessary skill and luck to make himself famous and accepted. There is a certain amount of competition among the Laibons, which is shown by the rivalry that may even go to such extremes as witchcraft, and comes to the fore especially when they are contending for the position of chief medicine man.

164 THE MUGWE, A FAILING PROPHET

Laibonhood, being open to any member of the Engi-dong clan, is not a true inheritance. It does not become a personal privilege by inheritance, but by personal efforts and achievements. On the other hand, the Ugwe is a power that is not only inherited within a lineage, but by a single person, totally and exclusively, so that only one candidate can be nominated and elected to the office of Mugwe.

The structural position of the chief Laibon is that of ' chief medicine man '. With regard to other Laibons, the emphasis is on his status as ' chief '. In relation to his tribe and people the stress remains on his profession as ' medicine man '. If we compare this with the status of the Mugwe the difference is considerable. The relationship of the Mugwe to his sub-tribe is much more intimate: he is the father of the people, the representative of God, the representative of his people to God and, by his mere presence among them, the guarantor of their continuity and prosperity. The Laibon is essentially a dispenser of charms and magic. Though he was regarded as a chief by the early Administration, it is now established that he was never considered to be such by his own people.

The functions of the Laibon, on the other hand, appear to be very similar, almost identical, with those of the Mugwe. The stress on rain-making, with regard to the Mugwe, is not as strong as with the Laibon; it certainly does not possess such a magical character. Only when the situation is desperate is the Mugwe asked to pray and offer sacrifices to God in order to obtain rain. With relation to the age-class system, the function of the Laibon, who authorizes the commencement of circumcision and blesses every new age-set and age-class, is exactly the same as that of the Mugwe. A further point of difference is also found in the way the Laibon and the Mugwe are related to the

THE POSITION OF THE MUGWE 165

age-classes. Though the Laibon authorizes the formation of the age-classes through their stages of initiation, he remains, so to speak, outside the inner structure of the class itself and his office is really entirely independent of the age-class. Indeed his authority over the age-classes is secondary to the authority of the *piron* elders and to that of the elders in general. With the Mugwe the situation is different, especially if we consider the system that obtains among the Igembe and the Tigania sub-tribes. There the Mugwe is expressed, as it were, by the age-class itself, and his period of office coincides with the period of power of the age-class that he blesses.

We may thus conclude that the Mugwe and the Laibon have the same functions within their own societies and can therefore be regarded as similar institutions, but there are real and considerable differences in their inner organization and in their structural position. The institution of the Mugwe is of a religious character while that of the Laibon is definitely of a ritual and magical nature. The Laibon, as Fosbrooke remarks, represents an institution 'not fully assimilated by the Masai organization'; the Mugwe, as an institution, has been completely accepted and has its full place in the structure of the Meru sub-tribe. The similarity of the functions of the two institutions and of the political organization of their societies, makes the political position of the two dignitaries very similar. The Masai and the Meru organizations are both based on the age-class system. The Laibon and the Mugwe control by their spiritual power, a control that they can exploit, if circumstances are favourable, in order to foster their own political aims.

(b) *The Hayu or Abba Boku of the Galla Boran*

Unfortunately there is no available description of the

166 THE MUGWE, A FAILING PROPHET

social structure of the southern Galla of Kenya who border on Meru. We shall, therefore, base the following comparison on the so-called ' normal type ' of the age-class system of the Galla Boran of South-West Abyssinia.

The age-class system, or *gada*-system, of the Boran is closely connected with the election of a dignitary called Hayu or Abba Boku or also Abba Gada. The title Abba Boku is derived from a sceptre, *boku*, that is presented to the Abba Boku, ' Father of the Sceptre ', at the time of his investiture; the other title, Abba Gada, is derived from the age-class system itself, *gada*, of which the Abba Gada becomes the Father, Abba, and the personification.

The age-class system of the Boran is organized into a series of five *gada*-sets or classes each extending over eight years. Within every age-class social status and political authority are reached and attained by passing through a series of five *gada*-grades each lasting eight years. The *gada*-grades are named as follows: Daballe, Folle, Qondala, Dori-Luba, Yuba. The Daballe do not nominate a Hayu. The Folle are the first to elect a Hayu, who is their leader. At his nomination he plants a ritual tree at the beginning and end of the grade-period. The next grade is divided into two stages of four years: Dori and Luba. It is during the latter stage that the class reaches its full political authority and governs the country. When the Dori stage is reached the Hayu, elected when the grade was Qondala, is formally invested. The Hayu is now Abba Boku or Abba Gada and assumes real political significance as the temporary chief and law-giver of the country for a period of eight years. He solemnly proclaims the laws of the country, which consists mainly of a repetition of the existing laws or the promulgation of new rulings. At this stage he again plants a ritual tree. During the next stage, Luba, the Abba Boku does not perform

THE POSITION OF THE MUGWE 167

any special ceremony, but rules the country by sitting in councils and giving judgment; he may also again make a solemn proclamation of the laws. Towards the end of the Luba stage, the Abba Boku and the members of the grade are circumcised, a ceremony that is regarded as a sign that they have left behind all political activities. At the end of the Dori-Luba grade, political authority is handed over to the next *gada*-set with its own Abba Boku. The final stage or grade, Yuba, marks the retiring stage. The Yuba elders no longer take part in the government of the country, except in an advisory capacity.

The above description gives a bare outline of the *gada*-system without considering the very many local differences, so that the structural position of the Hayu—Abba Boku may be seen clearly.

The election of the Abba Boku is made by the members of his own age-class and grade. He must be selected from among the families that supplied previous Abba Boku, so that the office is, very broadly, hereditary. Besides functioning as the law-giver, the Abba Boku presides over the tribal assemblies, and can also offer sacrifices, in which he is assisted by a ' ritual sister ', a young girl who is elected during the Qondala grade. The Abba Boku is also the head of the warriors, though in time of war his powers, as such, are delegated to the Abba Dula, the Father of the War.

The analogies between the Abba Boku and the Mugwe of the Meru, if they are considered generally, as in the above description of the *gada*-system, are quite striking. This becomes more evident if we consider the Mugwe institution in the system of the Igembe and the Tigania. The election of the Igembe Mugwe is primarily made by the members of the age-class, in a similar way to the election of the Abba Boku. The period of office of the two

168 THE MUGWE, A FAILING PROPHET

dignitaries likewise coincides with the period of office of their age-class. The political functions of the Abba Boku are much greater and his political character more stressed than those of the Mugwe. The Abba Boku proclaims the laws, rules the country and judges: there is no appeal against his sentences. The word of the Mugwe in a dispute is also final and there is no appeal, but this is due to his sanctioning power rather than to his function as a judge, a function that, as was noted, is only incidental to his office. The nomination of the Igembe Mugwe is also marked by the planting of ritual trees, a ceremony that plays such a prominent part in the *gada*-system and is so solemnly and repeatedly performed by the Hayu and the Abba Boku.

From the above comparative sketch, I do not think that we are entitled to draw any other conclusion than that there is a striking similarity between the institution of the Abba Boku and that of the Mugwe. The problem of the cultural relations between all the age-class systems so typical of the East-African zone, is still an open question which needs more material from the field and a thorough analysis of the structure, functions, and historical background.

A conclusion, however, that seems to be borne out by the above comparative analysis concerns the structural value of the institutions we have just examined. It seems that where the political system is based democratically on the age-class system, it requires or allows, at some point, the presence of an officer of higher, possibly supernatural or ritual, status who provides a sanctioning authority above the ordinary machinery of government, and beyond which there is no possible appeal. The office of such a dignitary serves to guarantee the orderly development of the country and the prosperity of the people.

Chapter Seven

THE FAILING PROPHET

I. CONCEALING THE MUGWE

When we consider the present position of the Mugwe there is no doubt that we are confronted with a decline. The sun, as it were, is sinking.

To put the main reason for this decline as simply and briefly as possible, one might say that it is the impact of the changing order. The phrase may be trite, but it describes the situation exactly. It has been fatal to the Mugwe and to the institution he stands for, that he has failed to present himself as something of permanent value on which new institutions might be built.

The situation is reflected in the elders and their attitude to the Mugwe. ' The house of the Mugwe cannot die ' is the saying that summarizes their emotional attitude to everything new. They simply cling to the past. It is pathetic to observe the way in which some of the elders loyally remain attached to their old ways, lamenting the changes that are taking place. The eventuality of an order of things entirely different from what they have known is excluded ' tout court ' by some of them. ' It is not possible,' stated one Imenti elder, ' that there should be no Mugwe. He will always be doing his work. Even if all his people should move from the country and not return, he would bless them by turning himself towards the direction of their migration, and his blessing would be carried by the wind. If he dies, another will take his place.'[1]

[1] It did not matter to this elder that there is at present no Mugwe among the Imenti. ' *Kiragu* is present,' he remarked, ' and even the Mugwe,

170 THE MUGWE, A FAILING PROPHET

Such an attitude has prompted attempts by the elders to resist the mounting tide. We know very little of these attempts because it is not an easy subject to talk about, consistently avoided or resisted and even resented. In spite of these difficulties I am convinced that there were definite attempts by the elders to conceal the Mugwe from the first Europeans and the Administration. That the elders suffered and were embittered by their patent impotence in halting what they thought to be the systematic dismantling of their old social and political structure is certain. Warriors were stopped from fighting, and though the initiates continued to be formed into sets and classes, these lost their old appeal and soon became obsolete and out of touch with the ideals of the new generations. Chiefs were imposed, regardless of the established order, and put there to stay, to collect taxes, to control movements, to change the old way of life.

The arrival of the Europeans is regarded as a turning point among the Meru—*Comba iji ni ijire*, ' the Europeans arrived '. The expression is idiomatic: *Comba* is an old term formerly used with reference to Arab travellers and traders from the coast who had introduced different ways of life. It is now applied to everything that has come to Meru with the Europeans, in other words ' the Europeans and all that '. There is in the expression a sense of frustration and disappointment due to the enforced adaptation to new ways.

The first arrival of the Europeans among the Meru has already entered the mythopoetical phase. I have recorded several narratives of those early days and it is significant to note how their tone reflects the character of the first white travellers and administrators. The following story

the one who will take hold of the *kiragu* in the near future is also there, a living man or a boy, though still unknown.'

THE FAILING PROPHET

was dictated to my assistant by an Imenti elder of Nkuene. It will be noted how the white men are not called by their own names, but by nicknames that were given to them by the Meru, a custom still followed.

When Kangangi came here we were young initiates, *nthaka*, and we went to meet him. He went first to a place called Kuurumwe, and then to Munithu where he sat in council with the elders; following this we started opening up the road.

Another one who came (after Kangangi) was cruel. He wounded and spoiled the hand of a man named M. Kajiru with his gun (lit. bullet, *mburuburu*). His house had been built inside the forest called *Kamacegi*, where he kept singing with his drums. This was his tune:

'The people of Kyanyaga are small boys, *ibieje*,
Ehe, the people of Kyanyaga are small boys.'

Now the men of Kyanyaga resented that, and they insulted him, and he killed a great number of them. If you ask the name of that man at your place at Kyanyaga I think you would be told that his name is Mwangia. He was indeed very bad, *kamucunku . . . gakathoku*.[1]

Other Europeans, *Comba*, came here while the Kubai were warriors. This age-set fought them fiercely. Probably there had been others before, and perhaps you have heard from your elders of the *Comba ya Mwangia*. Mwangia was in fact a Kamba interpreter of those Europeans, and that is the reason that the Meru called that bad European Mwangia.

The others are as follows: Githarike, Kereru, Rimanyangu, Kairethia. The house of Kairethia was near the road to Kaaga.

Kangangi was the first to arrive here, and when he arrived the Meru came under the British. With him all fighting was stopped and the country was at peace. No attackers ever came to this side. But there was no education as yet and the country was in great darkness, *nthiguru yari nunduni muno*. Before he

---

[1] *Mucunku* is a derivative term from the Swahili *Mzungu*, European, and is used by the Meru in a derogatory sense. The diminutive prefix *Ka* increases this sense as does the qualitative *gakathoku* rt. *thoku* bad, plus 2 reduplicative prefixes *gaka*, i.e. very, very bad, or mean.

172   THE MUGWE, A FAILING PROPHET

came here he was told by the Kikuyu that there was *nkuru*[1] in Meru. He came and found out the *nkuru* at Murathankari. Many people were killed but there was nothing that they could do. And he sent some of his askari. They went and saw some boys at Mutuate where there is now the school; and they killed them all. The men of Murathankari were very angry but there was nothing that they could do with the European. The pay of the askari was one bull and five goats and one blanket. Their leader was paid three goats.

There came other Europeans, but I do not know the work they did.

Another narrator, also from the Imenti, described Githarike as ill-treating the Imenti. One of his soldiers had been killed, it was said, by the Gitie; an expedition was sent against a *gaaru* of Nkomari, and many men were killed, and women also were killed between Kaongo and Igane. According to this narrator, Githarike was followed by Kangangi, whom he described as a good man who did not do any evil to the people.

Similar narrations were also recorded among the Tharaka. The Tharaka of Ntugi fought against one European and killed one of his askaris, and for that they lost a great number of goats and cattle. The story tells that the Mugwe did not know, or did not approve, of the attack.[2]

---

[1] *Nkuru* indicates a noisy group of initiates, *nthaka*, who roamed the country from house to house, compelling people to offer them food and meat. Not all the initiates were allowed to, or would willingly, join such a gang; only the most boisterous and violent among them. They were distinguished by a special cry, described as a horse's neigh, and a peculiar form of dancing. *Nkuru* could also refer either to the cry or to the form of dancing. The *nkuru* gang was greatly feared by all.

[2] Major G. St. J. Orde Brown states in his *The Vanishing Tribes of Kenya* that 'on several occasions (the Tharaka) made unprovoked attacks on Government Officials.' Also G. Lindblom in his work on the Akamba records ' the bellicose nature ' of the Tharaka. These are the only references to fighting between the early Europeans and the Meru sub-tribes. Having searched the files of the District Commissioner's office, Meru, I failed to find any record of these facts.

THE FAILING PROPHET   173

It is not possible, without records, to judge the historical accuracy of these stories. They do, however, illustrate the attitude of the elders and their resentment towards the first white men. It is unfortunate that these skirmishes should have occurred, because they have marred the early relations of the elders with the Administration, causing suspicion and resentment. Other rulings, such as the surrender of all shields, were also greatly resented.

It was only natural, therefore, that as soon as the elders convinced themselves that their very existence as a people was at stake, they tried to protect the man who was the symbol of their prosperity and continuity. The actions of men like Githarike, as recorded in the above narrations, took place in the area where the Mugwe of the Imenti had his residence. There is no doubt that they caused great fear and suspicion and can be logically considered as, at least partly, responsible for the retiring attitude and elusiveness of the Mugwe. Indeed, from that time on, the Mugwe and all matters connected with him were surrounded by secrecy and mystery, a policy which seems to have been followed consistently, especially among the Imenti and the Tharaka. When I enquired among the Tharaka why the Mugwe had been surrounded by so much unjustified secrecy, I was answered: 'We were afraid that they would kill him.'

'The Mugwe has been lost,' stated an elder of the Imenti, 'because of the white man. They said that *kiragu* was poison, and the one who held it was told that he would be removed from the country.' The obvious interpretation of this statement would seem to suggest a direct attack by the Administration on the Mugwe of Imenti. In the light of similar information, and bearing in mind the history of the Orkoyot of the Nandi and Kipsigis and the Laibon of the Masai, I made enquiries at the District Commissioner's

174 THE MUGWE, A FAILING PROPHET

Office in Meru and they very kindly allowed me to search through their files. Nothing came to light. In fact the absolute silence of the files on the Mugwe and his relationship to the age-class system, made it evident that the very existence of the Mugwe had entirely escaped the attention of the Administration.

The words ' they said it was poison ' might, perhaps, be explained by reference to the successful fight waged against witchcraft by the Administration in Meru in the early years.[1] If this is true, it would also mean that the Mugwe was taken to be merely one of the many witches who used their medicines and poisons to exploit people's credulity.

It is also possible that the Mugwe, having had some connection with the armed resistance of the Tharaka to the early Officers, or with other similar armed actions, was afterwards protected and hidden from all the investigations that followed the reprisals or other punitive measures.

2. CHANGING ATTITUDES

The complaints of the elders are caused by their comparison of the new way of life with the old standards, generally to the detriment of the former. Remarks concerning the younger generation and things in general are very common. ' You are not as we were,' stated an elder to my assistant, ' you always quarrel, and the reason is that you do not respect your elders.' ' This is the power of the machine-guns, *unene bwa micinka*,' stated another Imenti elder, ' but at the time of the Mugwe we would have been happy without guns. The young initiates were

---

[1] A number of secret societies, the *athi*, the *kagita*, etc., were outlawed Their character was secret because they were addicted to making and distributing poisons. Their houses were burnt down for the last time during the year 1926.

THE FAILING PROPHET 175

told to behave properly; the elders were expected to do the actions of elderhood and not of childhood. The only man who had to suffer in those days was the one who did not want to do like the others. We say that if our chief, *munene*—the Mugwe, would come back, we would not like to be dominated by the present state of affairs, *comba iji iri ku nandi.*'

The consequence of the Mugwe's concealment was first detrimental to the Ugwe itself as an institution. The very existence of the Mugwe became an esoteric subject known only to the elders. It is indeed amazing to realize how the great majority of the youth of Meru, those who would have been warriors in the old age-class-system, do not know anything about the Mugwe. Most of my pupils at Nkubu learnt of his existence from me.

The attitude of his people to the Mugwe has, thus, been gradually changing into one of indifference, disbelief and even contempt. *Antu nandi ni bakumena Mugwe* ' People now despise (do not acknowledge) the Mugwe,' stated M. Kamunde. And M. Kiganka of the Chuka complained, ' They no longer believe in me! '

The main form of the Mugwe's activity, blessing the age-classes and controlling their activities, had come to a standstill when its function had been disrupted by the prohibition of raids and by the uselessness of a defending army. The initiates were left to fend for themselves, while there was no substitute to replace their old activity. The beginning of formal education came slowly and, in any case, was necessarily limited to the few. The lack of the old discipline brought the country into a bad state: *nthiguru yathukiri ni untu bwa kwaga gaaru,* ' the country went wrong because there were no more *gaaru* '. *Gaaru* has a comprehensive meaning, including the training and the discipline of the initiates. Some elders contrast the

176 THE MUGWE, A FAILING PROPHET

present life of the young people with their own, as in the following statement by an Imenti elder: ' But now, look at us: we are of one age-class, Riungu, we are of one way of life (lit. habit, *muturiri jumwe*), that we received from the Mugwe: only if a man is a bad man, would he refuse to follow that way of life.'

Though many elders cling to their past, not all the elders think in this way. Even those who sometimes complain are quite ready at other times to admit that new things are good. ' When you become an old man,' said an Imenti elder to my assistant, ' you will be able to get many things, even treatment for your sick cows. You will have medicines for yourself, and you will be able to eat food without any pain. Your life will not be as difficult as this life of ours. Also, if some of you will not be rich— for there are poor in every country—you have already learned to assist one another and, having learned that, you will follow that custom till your death.'

Since the first arrival of the Europeans, other specialized agencies have entered the arena, trying to change for the better the mind and the soul of the Meru. Formal education at school and the spreading of the Gospel attracted the loyalty of an ever-increasing number of young men who, because of their new allegiance, had no more interest in the Mugwe and the old way of life, even after their initiation into manhood. Schools became centres of social intercourse, at which boys and men from various different sub-tribes came together, so that a sense of tribal unity over and above the sub-tribal level was being continually fostered. Such a tendency has also been encouraged by Administration. Indeed, it is a natural consequence of all the sub-tribes being administered within a single District. The process of tribal unification has been growing and spreading throughout the years until, recently, it was

THE FAILING PROPHET

officially established by the proclamation of Meru as an independent Land Unit. It is not that sectional divisions and differentiations have been entirely effaced, but they are certainly no longer as parochial and particular as they used to be.

In the past, the position of the Mugwe was paramount in each sub-tribe and had, therefore, a sectional character that was somehow reconciled by the abstraction of the power of the Ugwe as something single and unique for all the Meru. At present, however, against the background of an ever-increasing tribal, or even 'Kenyan' consciousness, the position of the Mugwe is bound to be looked upon as something entirely obsolete with no constructive value for the present progressive generation.

The situation, as it now stands, is intimately connected with the personality of the living Agwe. Indeed, the survival of the institution, for better or for worse, is conditioned by the force or the weakness of these personalities. The following brief survey of the individual position of the living Agwe will bear this out.

3. M. KIGANKA OF THE CHUKA

In the course of the foregoing descriptions I have had the chance of quoting some illustrative statements by M. Kiganka, the Mugwe of the Chuka, all of which indicate a very strong personality.

When I first met M. Kiganka, I was left with the impression of a broken man, for Fate had been hard on him. He was good enough to give me his friendship and confidence and, when he realized that my interest in him and the Ugwe was genuine, and that I could be trusted, the vitality, strength, and courage that he showed in his efforts to regain his position were indeed tremendous. He never wavered and stood up bravely to his fate.

178   THE MUGWE, A FAILING PROPHET

I have already mentioned how M. Kiganka asked for my assistance in a curious predicament. He had conceived the idea of approaching the Mugwe of the Igembe in order to recover at least some of his lost things of the Ugwe. A similar co-operation between the two Agwe had already taken place in the past when the Igembe had found themselves in equally serious distress. There had been a severe drought in Igembe, and the spectre of famine was looming ahead. Cattle were dying and men also. It was then that the Mugwe of the Igembe approached the Mugwe of the Chuka begging for his assistance. The Mugwe of Chuka sent his staff, and by this the Igembe recovered their prosperity. (Other Chuka elders in a previous interview had stated that it was the Tigania who ' at a time when they had no cattle because they were all dying, came (to Chuka) to get the Ugwe '. I was unable to establish which of the two versions was the true one, but I gave credit to M. Kiganka, as Mugwe, and followed his version.)

It was September 1955. The Emergency regulations were strictly enforced and all movements by Africans were controlled by pass regulations, and, in any case, greatly discouraged. On my advice, M. Kiganka dictated the following message which I took on myself duly to deliver to the Mugwe of the Igembe.

Mugwe Igembe,

M. Kiganka, Mugwe uria uri Chuka, nkwenda gukinyia kuu ni untu bwa ukuru nuntu ni ndaithirwe mucii na into biakwa bionthe, na mwana wakwa akirutwa ni Mau Mau

To the Mugwe of the Igembe,

From M. Kiganka, the Mugwe of Chuka. I want to come to you on account of the elderhood, because my house and all my property have been burnt down, and my son has been carried off

THE FAILING PROPHET

mucii akiuragirwa njirene rutere rwa ruji.

Maukuru jau ni jo nkwenda gukinyia kuu o mbere, ni untu into biakwa bia Ugwe bionthe ni biaithirue buru. Kiu ni kio gitumi mpenda gukinya kuu, umpe into kithira gwe utaithirwa kana kithira nutigaritie into biu.

Nkwenda wethirwa utigaritie, ungaire nuthu kethira bururi yakwa ikomba gucoa bingi.

Riu ninkwenda wandike baruga, umbire riria mpumbikia gukinya kuu amwe na Chief Isaia M. Imanene. Wenda ncokagiria baruga iji na mpui muno ni untu ndi na thina.

Riu ni ngugucokeria nkatho muno. Ni ndienda gukinya kuu tweriganita.

Ni nii, Mugwe, Chuka,
M. Kiganka wa M. Kanata.

from the house by the Mau Mau and killed on the road on the side of the river.

These matters of the elderhood are the reason why I want to come to you in the first place, because all my things of the Ugwe have been destroyed altogether.

That is the reason why I want to come to you in the first place, so that you give me the things, if yours have not been burnt and if you have any left.

In case they are not finished give me a little (lit. half) of them. (to see) whether my territory may not be able to find the rest. Now, I want you to write a letter and say when I may come there together with Chief Isaia M. Imanene. Please, give an early answer to this letter, because I am suffering.

And now I wish to thank you very much. I would not like to come and then not meet you.

It is I, the Mugwe of the Chuka,
M. Kiganka M. Kanata.

The above letter is couched in a characteristic style. The first reason given by M. Kiganka for his writing is

180   THE MUGWE, A FAILING PROPHET

' the elderhood '. ' To know the things of the elderhood ' is an expression that we have noted beforehand; it implies respect, consideration and proper treatment of the elders. It is therefore a compliment paid in order to open the way to the main subject.

The Mugwe of the Chuka wants to consult the Mugwe of the Igembe about the situation, and possibly to adopt similar measures in Chuka which were being followed in Igembe, if they were really effective ('if yours have not been burnt '), and if they could be taken and applied to Chuka (' give me a little '), or just to see whether the Chuka could solve the situation by themselves (' whether my territory may not be able to find the rest ').

The mention of Chief Isaia, the Chief of the Chuka, was suggested, I think, by the elders in order to make things easier and to assure the elders of Igembe that, if the visit was to take place, it would have been in full accordance with the Emergency regulations.

It was only a few weeks afterwards that I was able to deliver the letter to M. Mugambi of the Igembe at Antubociu. Naturally, he was flattered by the message, but he would not commit himself and asked for time to consult with the elders. The answer came later, and was in the negative, given only verbally. The Mugwe of the Igembe and the elders became rather reticent; they stated that they had nothing to do with the Mugwe of the Chuka. I was left with the impression that the Mugwe and elders of the Igembe were afraid of becoming involved in a serious commitment at a time when everything was going wrong because of the Emergency. Perhaps the very mention of the chief's name in M. Kiganka's letter had been sufficient to arouse their suspicion.[1]

---

[1] During my stay in Meruland I had repeated experiences of a similar attitude by the elders. My field work took place while the Mau

THE FAILING PROPHET 181

When I met M. Kiganka after this, he had no comment; he looked sad and I respected his silence.

I saw him again recently at his traditional place near Chera. He had recovered some confidence, but the general situation was much the same, and the trend of the people still away from him.

4. THE VACANCY IN IMENTI

In the past the fame of the Imenti Mugwe was certainly very great. It is evident from the vivid memories preserved by the elders which I was able to record. I have observed with the greatest interest some elders become excited while recalling the past glories of the Mugwe of Kirirwa. It was, therefore, the more disappointing, and to some extent surprising, to realize the odd situation that exists in Imenti with regard to the Ugwe. There is no Mugwe at present, for 'no one was willing to take the place of the last one'. Mention has been made above of some of the reasons that might have been responsible for this fear of taking up the Ugwe heritage. I may add here that there were three consecutive deaths in the house of M. Ngitira, the man who, according to the elders, should have been the Mugwe. I am unable to say how much influence these tragic happenings had on the decision of M. Ngitira to refuse the Ugwe. The fact that they were mentioned in connection with his refusal seems to indicate that they were regarded as a kind of legal impurity, or something of the sort, making it unsafe for M. Ngitira or anyone else of his house to become Mugwe.

Mau Emergency was strictly in force. Whenever I had to introduce myself to one or other of the elders, breaking the ice was always difficult. There was a patent suspicion that my presence was in some way connected with Government, and that I had come there to observe their attitude to the Mau Mau and to control their movements. In a very few cases, indeed, I was unable to overcome such suspicions and had to turn away and look for some other man or place. Generally, however, when my assistant had made plain who I was, the attitude of the elders became friendly and open.

182   THE MUGWE, A FAILING PROPHET

As I have pointed out, all things, places, and persons related to the Ugwe in the area of Kirirwa still inspire great awe and respect. But the elders of the Mugwe's house are not prepared to say much. When the subject turns on the present vacancy of the Mugwe, they simply say: ' Well, *kiragu* is still preserved, and another Mugwe will arise sometime.'

There is no doubt, however, that though the *kiragu* is still preserved, to people in general and especially to young people *kiragu* has become meaningless, even when its existence is known. It is, as it were, a hidden treasure, an intriguing secret, of which the elders may sometimes be induced to speak, but which is becoming more and more forgotten.

If the area of Kirirwa is excepted, I think that I am correct in saying that among the Imenti the Mugwe is, in effect, a figure of the past, and that the Ugwe, as an institution, has lost its significance with the people and its influence on the social structure.

5. THE MUGWE OF THE THARAKA

Of all Meru, the Tharaka have remained most detached in their mode of life. There are many reasons for this. Their country is ecologically quite different from the rest of Meru, being low-lying, hot and somewhat unfertile. Residentially they are cut off from the other sub-tribes, whose markets they visit regularly by walking long distances, especially during their recurrent periods of famine. Goats, cattle, and sheep are bartered for all kinds of cereals. The isolation of their country is also one of the reasons why, up to a very short time ago, there has been little activity among them by the Agricultural and Medical Departments: in the whole country there was only one Dispensary, run by an African dresser. A mobile clinic from the Catholic Mission, Imenti, paid regular visits

THE FAILING PROPHET 183

every week, until a missionary station was opened at
Materi, north of the Mutonga River, in the year 1956.
Though the Seventh Day Adventists have run a primary
school for some years, this remained outside the Government plan for African education. Only during and after
the Emergency has the school system been expanded
among the Tharaka.

Thus, it might be expected that the position of the
Mugwe of the Tharaka would still have some significance,
if not as much as in the olden days, and would at least
have some real influence on Tharaka social life. Indeed it
is partly so, for the Mugwe still controls the initiation,
which can take place only after the circumciser's knives
have been blessed by him and proper fees have been paid
to him. But, except for this small field of control, the
Mugwe is becoming more and more remote from the
interests and ideals of the young Tharaka.

I have observed M. Ruanda in his movements to and
from his house and Chokarige Market. He is certainly
very much respected, especially by the elders, but his
contact with the new generation is negligible. The elders,
and M. Ruanda himself, complained of the fact. M.
Ruanda also complained that very few elders go to him
nowadays, and that he has been generally abandoned.
This was a direct consequence of the terminating of the
warriors' activities and the decline of the *gaaru* system. It
was a result of the new allegiance that people were asked
to give to the appointed chief. But there were other causes.
The Tharaka of Urio section gradually lost their sense of
affiliation to the Mugwe. There was also a lack of
personality in the present Mugwe. During my last visit
to Tharaka, when I had already met M. Kiganka of
Chuka, I could not help comparing the two men and
noticing the great difference between them. M. Ruanda is

184 THE MUGWE, A FAILING PROPHET

certainly conscious of his dignity as Mugwe, in the same way that M. Kiganka is. But he is slow in thinking and weak in action. He lacks that warmth that made M. Kiganka appear like a giant in his misfortune. In my experience I found that the elders of the Tharaka were more vigorous in trying to retain their Ugwe than M. Ruanda himself, so that the neglect he complains of must be ascribed in part to his own retiring attitude.

6. THE MUGWE OF THE IGEMBE AND OF THE TIGANIA

Until recently the 'immobility' of the people of the Nyambeni Range and their lack of interest in modern developments was regarded almost as one of their characteristics. Both the Tigania and the Igembe have remained attached to their old systems and way of life unlike some of the other Meru sub-tribes. Old institutions such as the age-class system still function in a somewhat orthodox form, keeping the time-rhythms of open and closed periods of initiation. The power of the elders is very great, as it is nowhere else in Meru, since the association of the *njuri* is most effective in this area, and the system of grades and councils is still maintained. The efforts of the Administration to absorb the *njuri* into the administrative system of Meru gave new strength to their association and the continuance of the *njuri* as a governing body is partly due to this.

A singular consequence of this strengthening of the *njuri* is the co-existence in Igembe, and also in Tigania, of the old system of government, still somehow functioning, and the administrative system of chiefs and headmen. It is true that such a duality of authority is not entirely absent in other Meru sub-tribes, but nowhere in Meru are the elders so strongly organized as in Igembe and Tigania.

Against this background the position of the Mugwe and

THE FAILING PROPHET 185

of the Mukiama cannot but be of practical importance in the social system.

The survival of initiation and of the age-sets in their traditional form, though with the warriors' activity curtailed, has meant a continuity of the power and function of the Mugwe. The intimate connection of the Mugwe with the formation of the age-classes among both the Tigania and the Igembe is another reason for his continuing.

Evidently the abolition of the warriors as such did not, among the Tigania and the Igembe, have the same negative effect on the structure of their society as among the other sub-tribes. The strength of the *njuri* association and the hold that they still have on their people, are the main reasons for this phenomenon. Entry into the *njuri* association is by invitation, but this invitation may be extended only to initiates. In my opinion, therefore, the attraction offered by warriorhood in the olden days has been replaced by that still afforded by *njuri* membership and by newly initiated *njuri*, who wander around the country with their faces painted and decorated with esoteric patterns whose significance is known only to the initiates.

There is, however, another side of the picture. During the last few years, even on the Nyambene Range, there have been some noticeable developments. Interest in education has greatly increased; there are now two intermediate schools, and more are planned. The number of educated young men is still small, but they have aligned themselves with the other young Meru by their attraction towards progress and civilization and have lost their attachment to the old way of life. I know of young educated men who have resisted all invitations to join the *njuri* (even by the new method of a Christian oath), not because they did not want to serve their country, nor because they could not

186   THE MUGWE, A FAILING PROPHET

afford to pay the high fees demanded, but because they felt that it was a form of association they could no longer support, having convinced themselves that they were able to serve their country more effectively by following other, more progressive, forms of association.

Instances of a similar attitude are to be found even in the house of the Mugwe of the Igembe. The eldest son of M. Mugambi, M. Ithiria, is at present a teacher in a school and he has expressed his intention of being baptized a Roman Catholic. Recently, during the most recent *ntuiko*, I was informed that the interest of young men in this ' old fashioned ' festivity was not great, and the elders made much more of it than the young men.

It appears, therefore, that the structural position of the Mugwe, which had held its own up to now, is being undermined by the increasing effects of civilization which are slowly but surely, being felt by the people of the Nyambene Range.

7. DIFFERENT REACTIONS TO THE PRESENT CHANGES

While it is evident that among all the Meru the influence of the Mugwe is fast declining, it is significant to note how the *mugaa* is able to hold his own in spite of the changing situation. This is, I think, due to the different structural values of the two institutions.

The Mugwe is a public dignitary with official authority, intimately connected with the old social structure, which is now undergoing very deep and thorough changes. The source of authority, of political authority extending over the whole of society, is now quite outside the old structural institutions. Authority is, therefore, differently distributed and differently held. It is not supernaturally bestowed, nor is it inherited or attained by social progress in the age-class system. It

THE FAILING PROPHET 187

is under the absolute control of the Administration which appoints and dismisses chiefs and headmen according to their efficiency. As the old structure decays, so does the authority of the Mugwe. Such a decline cannot, or could not, have been sudden, but it is, nonetheless, a process which has developed as quickly as the changes brought about by the new structural agencies which have entered the life of the Meru people with the coming of the Administration.

The *mugaa*, on the other hand, is a private practitioner; he is not so intimately bound up with the structure of his society to which he offers the benefits of his art. As an art, his activity remains unaffected by structural changes. It can only be opposed by another, superior, art. But though the eventual issue is certain long before it can be realized, there is no doubt that any new art that is offered as a substitute for the old one, must begin by changing the mentality and old beliefs on which the old practice prospers. All this presupposes a change of mind, clearly much more difficult and taking much longer than any change of structure which can be controlled and directed from the outside, as it were, by force of an administrative authority. It follows that the *mugaa* has been practically undisturbed by the many alterations forced upon Meru social structure by the new authority. He still continues to be consulted as a private practitioner by private clients. It is also not unusual to discover that educated men have had recourse to the medicine-man.

The *mugaa* has also gained some advantages from the recession of the Mugwe. On matters on which it would have been proper for the elders to consult with the Mugwe, they now turn to the *mugaa*, who still represents for them a living link with their past in all its functions. This is a further reason why the new generations know more about

188 THE MUGWE, A FAILING PROPHET

the *mugaa*, whom they may see daily about their houses, than they do about the Mugwe.

At this stage, the figure of the Mugwe, as the representative of God among his people, a leader of his people, as tutor of young initiates, as guarantor of his society's prosperity, as ' Father ', as ' God ', and as the holder of an office requiring extraordinary moral virtues, might stand out as something ideal and removed from reality. We have noted, however, that the descriptions of some of the living, and also of some of the past Agwe have afforded instances indicating their human frailty and shortcomings. Moreover, it should be recalled that the distinction between the Mugwe as a public man in high office and the Mugwe as a private man is consistently made by the elders. There is no doubt, as we have said, that the Mugwe was not, in the mind of his people, a divine incarnation, but simply a man exalted to a very high position in the structure of his society and in the mind of the ordinary man.

His main functions were to bless and to sanction. That such a high ideal of moral life (even where that ideal was only to remain an abstract standard) should have been a requisite of his high office, says much for the natural moral values of the Meru.

The present decline of the Mugwe is inherent in the nature of things. The new order does not require a sanctioning officer outside the established authority, and the Mugwe has not shown himself capable of being adapted to this structure. In any case, his work of blessing cannot be divorced from the old structure, and there is, therefore, no suitable place for the Mugwe in the new society. This is the basic reason for the present decline of the institution as such.

THE FAILING PROPHET 189

The elders have developed an emotional attitude towards their past and towards the Mugwe. But it is not difficult to foresee that, whatever moral authority the Mugwe still wields at the present, it will very soon have vanished.

Such an outstanding institution of Meru society should not be allowed to die out without being recorded, and that has been the aim of this present work, which I have also felt as an obligation to the younger Meru generation.

THE END

APPENDIX

SOME SELECT DOCUMENTS AND NARRATIONS

1. ABOUT MBWA. By M. Kaboto, told to my assistant.

We all hear that we came out from Mbwa but there is no one among us who might know where this land called Mbwa is situated.

Our fathers and also their ancestors had not seen it, but we hear from the tradition (*ni untu rukari ja rugono*), we hear that it exists.

We are told that we came out from the land of north (*rutiri rwa urio*). We crossed that water that is called *Mbweni*. There was one of our elders who was our chief. I cannot remember his name, but I think that perhaps it was *Mairanyi*. At that time he had his staff and his knife.

When we arrived at that water he stopped and we also stopped. He said: 'Now you, we have arrived at the water (*iriene*) and we cannot cross; what can we do so that we may cross?'

They did not answer because he was the leader, and he could do what he liked. Then he said: 'Let us settle on this side of the river; let us stay here; let us graze our cattle; let us stay and live happily.'

But his people were not pleased because they were suffering greatly, and there was nothing that they could do. So they said: 'We cannot die here, it is better for us to cross even if we have to die in it.'

So he said to them: 'Those who have their children on their back let them put themselves in order; those who wear shoes, let them take them off; and those who are pregnant let them be careful.' When he finished those words, he said with a loud voice: 'Water divide yourself, so that my children may cross.' He said this four times. And women were shrieking at a high pitch.

192 THE MUGWE, A FAILING PROPHET

At the fourth time, they saw the water swelling and raising itself, and they were very much afraid. And again they saw the water swelling and raising itself, and they saw, but they could not understand how, dry soil between the waters.

Their leader said: ' Let a small girl and a small boy come here. First the small girl and then the small boy.' And then he said: ' Now enter into the water and cross.'

And the chief now said: ' Let a young woman (*ngutu*) and a young man (*ntani*) cross the water.' And they crossed.

After that he said: ' Now all must cross, but I shall go first.' He entered the water and he crossed and all his people followed him and they all crossed.

When they had finished crossing, the two large walls that had been formed by the water, merged slowly together until the water was as before.

Having arrived in the desert, they said: ' Now there is nothing that we can do because we are all the clans together. So let the clans divide themselves according to their will.'

This was the place where people separated from each other. We came this side and we arrived at Lake Baringo; we divided from the Turkana, the Jaluo and the Lumbwa and from the others who went by themselves.

2. THE TRADITION OF THE CHUKA. By four Elders of Chuka: Kararwa M. Amwarari, M. Rendiri M. Rutere, M. Mbwani Mukira, Mugira M. Njuki.

Long ago the people of Chuka lived in the forest in order to protect themselves from their attackers. Our forefathers came from the forest, but we know that there are others who came from Mbwa. The Gumba used to be here. Long ago the Chuka had their Mugwe. The Gumba had no Mugwe of their own but, according to what we heard, the Mugwe used to stay with them in the same way as he lives with us now.

The Mugwe made people prosper; therefore he could not do anything wrong. The Mugwe is like the Kabaka of Uganda, or like the Bishop who performs the Mass. When there was a fight or a war he told his son to take the lead.

It was the Mugwe who told us to come out of the forest on

APPENDIX

193

account of our attackers. The Tigania, the Mbere, the Kikuyu, were our enemies. The Igembe were our friends on account of *giciaro*.

The actions of the Mugwe are very good and beneficial to his people. The Mugwe of the Chuka uses his own honey-beer, sheep and rams and dons his own mantle for the day when he 'takes out' a new age-class into the field. On that day everybody is very pleased and they enjoy themselves by dancing for him. This Mugwe 'took out' *Miriti* who are now the young initiates, and also *Karia* were taken out by him. After this Emergency people will again gather together and go to see him.

All the people of Chuka will gather at Chera, all will go there, all the age-classes, also from Magumoni, and from Rogucha though it is on the border of Tharaka.

Once when the Tigania lost their cattle, they came here to ask for the Ugwe. At that time *Micubu* were initiated. They came here in order to be told what to do. And now we wanted to go there and we could not because of Mau Mau.

The Ugwe is one: To look after the country, to look after the seeds so that the people may be happy. Before circumcision is performed, the Mugwe has to bless the circumciser's knife; before anyone is allowed to circumcise, the Mugwe must have given his permission. It is he who says to all the Chuka: 'Now you can circumcise.'

When a man is sick he cannot be blessed by the Mugwe. It is only the people of his own clan that can be blessed by the Mugwe. Not all of them can go to him but only the elders.

When there is no rain or things are going badly, it is he who knows what to do. The first thing he asks them to do is to kill a sheep and eat it all up. When the Mugwe blesses his people, these become very happy. The first thing he says is: 'I want my country to be well.'

3. 'ALL OF US ARE ONE'. Dictated by M. Iboto, recorded by Cornelio M. Mbijiwe.

All peoples came from the same place. But the first to be born was a black man, and after him a white man [lit. *umutune*, red]

194 THE MUGWE, A FAILING PROPHET

was born. Then they started quarelling as between brothers.

A girl was also born, and her name was *Bong'ina* (' Of-the-mother '). It was for her that they started quarrelling. And a black man shouted: ' We shall go away.' And they heard it, ' We shall go away.' And all said: ' Now we go away.'

Some warriors were sent to look where to cross to the other side of the sea.

They stayed away for many days. They lighted fires and, having seen that, they said: ' Let us forge a spear.' They came and said: ' We did not find a crossing.' And off they went.

But God said: ' Go, because I want to speak to you.' God came, he stroked the water with his staff and the sea divided so that we could pass.

There were men who came and asked: ' How could these pass through that water? '

Now, these are the names by which they were called afterwards: 'black', 'red', 'white'. The black are those who came out during the night; the red are those who came out at dawn; the white came out in the full light of the day.

We arrived here, we came here, and we did not have any trouble as we had before we left.

When they (the white men) had been left by themselves, they started making all their things that you see, boats, planes, etc. which they used in order to come here. Now that they have come, there is nothing they cannot do. And now we suffer. Don't you see some of your friends in the forest?

But God knows that we came out all together. Look at that saliva [he had just spat]: there are some water parts [i.e. black spots], and there are some white parts; but all of them came out from the same place, to show that we should not be divided.

All of us are one, all are one.

4. THE TAIL OF THE MUGWE. Recorded by Teacher SAMWEL M. MUGANA.

Now we shall hear about a man called Mugwe. He is from

APPENDIX   195

Chokarige and he has lived there since long ago. This man is
respected by all the Tharaka, the Tharaka of Chokarige and
the Tharaka of Gatue, and the reason is that he was not born
like all other men, for he has got a tail like the animals. He is
the man who blesses the people. When they want to circumcise their sons they must ask his permission and he will bless
the knives by spitting on them. Only a few specialized men
(the circumcisers) can use these knives.

This wonderful thing not everybody can see with their own
eyes, not a young initiate not even some of the elders, but they
have only heard with their ears. Only the elders of renown,
who go there twice or thrice in the year, have seen him and he
blesses them. These elders who have seen, it is they who come
and tell the others about all these things. In Gatue only one
hundred elders have seen the Mugwe.

5. THE MUGWE IS OUR GOD—HIS CARE FOR THE
INITIATES. By M. Magiri M. Kiraithe of Ngonyi, Imenti.

You know that there was no other man that we respected more
than the one called Mugwe.

The Mugwe we called also our God. The reason why we
called him our God was that whatever we wanted he did for
us. He despised nobody. For instance when we wanted to go
to raid the Embu it was he who gave us advice to go. There
could be no man who could offend us by the name ' *maitha* '
(thieves). We were allowed only to raid (cattle).

You know that, even now, there are people who do not
want to keep the orders of Government. Such people are
punished according to their mistakes. In the same way if some
went to raid without the Mugwe's blessing they were punished:
sometimes they were killed on the road by other people, other
times they were killed by wild animals, and only if God helped
them to return home, then would the Mugwe also spare them.
He would spare them in this way: whenever there is famine, it
fell upon them (those who had sinned) to go and get food from
far countries for the initiates in the *gaaru*.

During those raids they could not suffer any defeat, because

o*

they had the blessing of the Mugwe. Such men would no longer make mistakes, because their punishment was indeed heavy. From here to Embu it was a long journey, but they could stand it because they knew it was the order of the Mugwe, and they could not avoid it.

He (the Mugwe) gave them the order in the presence of all the elders: ' You are useless for you did not keep my command. Now your job is heavier than that of any other: go to look for food for these children who have no legs (who cannot walk) and cannot go far (because recently circumcised). That is your punishment.'

On such occasions the Mugwe showed his greatness because he looked after the well-being of the young initiates by sending people to supply food for them. He did not abandon them while they were in their shelter (*iganda*).

6. WHO IS MUGWE. By RUCAORU of Materi, Tharaka.

The Mugwe is called Mugwe because he is the man who says ' This tree will die,' and that tree dies. Such is the Mugwe. His work is to bless the knives before they can be used for circumcision, and for that he possesses a staff. He also has a mantle which will pass on to his son.

I saw Mutuampea. We went there to be blessed, all of us of my age-set, who were initiated together, for we were the new set. His blessing was as follows: ' Go (work hard), do not stop on the road, and you will earn and prosper.'

It is the Europeans who stopped people from going to the Mugwe to be blessed.

The Mugwe, of course, was married, but he never goes with other men's women.

The clan of the Mugwe is *Kithuri*, it is a clan of power (*unene*), but it is not only of the Mugwe. People of this clan do not curse, nor do they do evil things. They came out of the waters, and one man called Kithuri said: ' I am of Kithuri, no one can dare to do evil.'

These people of Kithuri started to bore stones and to stretch hides over the stones. They also taught how to put oil

APPENDIX 197

in the fields when there was no rain. For these great things of the beginning they possess great power (*unene*).

7. WHEN WE VISITED THE MUGWE. By M. KAMUNDE, Chokarige.

The Mugwe can do something for the rain, but we do not know exactly, for we never go near him as we respect him greatly because he is our chief from the beginning.

To visit the Mugwe people went with all their lineages.

When a man is poisoned he can be taken by other people to the Mugwe but not before his permission has been obtained. A man cannot go by himself to the Mugwe; he must go with many others and offer him many things: a goat, a ram, some honey, some beer and other food.

When people go to see the Mugwe there will be plenty of food; women give birth to many children, even those who were barren.

When we used to go to see the Mugwe, we were very many, and we had very many things, rams, sheep, beer, honey— many, many things. For the occasion we wore our own clothes only, but the initiates carried also their own insignia such as the shield, the sword, the spear, the stick, and many other things.

We went to visit the Mugwe whenever our families were not prospering.

Those who were coming from far were given hospitality in his compound. In the morning he blessed them all, saying:

Borugea into bibiingi,	' Get many things,
boruciara antu babaingi,	beget many children,
bati ncai	who are without blemish,
batikwajwa,	who do not become sick,
bururi mauki jamaingi muno,	get honey in plenty,
bogea na irio bibiingi muno	get food in plenty,
bia kuriraga twana,	to feed your children,
na bogea na mburi iri na arethi.	and get sheep with their shepherds.'

198 THE MUGWE, A FAILING PROPHET

8. THE POWER AND THE BENEFITS OF THE MUGWE.
By M. MUGA, Chokarige.

If the country were not with the Mugwe it could not go on as well as before, for the man who is strong would start stealing things from the others. But now, because the Mugwe is there, a man goes to him to report.

The honey of the Mugwe is there and cannot be finished. The elders are there to see that it does not finish. That honey is not of his own benefit only, it is for all his people. If that honey were to finish, he himself and his country would perish with it: all the Tharaka would be destroyed and also his own lineage. In Imenti they have *kiragu*. This honey, this is what we call *kiragu*.

The Mugwe is not of a special age-class, and he is not of a special clan: he is of all his country, for he does not separate his sons from the others.

The reason why people say that the Mugwe is not of a single clan is the following: if his son does something wrong he has to treat him in the same way as he does the others. That is the reason. He is of no clan, because he is the chief of all. Now there is the white man who rules: does he govern one land and hate another?

His power is of all his clan because they must be present whenever he performs. But it is he who is the chief. He is the chief also of his own clan and of all the elders of that clan. That is the reason why that clan is so greatly feared.

9. THE MUGWE AND HIS PEOPLE. By M. MUGWERIA M.
KIRIA of Ntakira, Imenti.

Our Mugwe was a very good man because he advised his people and played *kiothi* [African draughts] with them. He played *kiothi* always. He did not do any other work but playing. His fields were cultivated by his people and they also gave him food.

At harvesting time when there was so much food, and when everybody was so happy, they went to him to sing and dance. From this he could see which were the good and the bad.

APPENDIX 199

Sitting at his place he observed them carrying their gifts to him. On coming to him they sang. Their songs were very happy. Also the Mugwe was very happy. The fences around his house had been erected by his people.

10. KIRAGU AND THE AGWE. (By the same man.)

Another thing is that every Mugwe knows the other Mugwe. The Mugwe of Chuka, of Tharaka, all of them say that they are one. The Mugwe of Igembe and of Tigania say that they are the same. All of them have got their *kiragu*. *Kiragu* is the Ugwe. When you hear the Mugwe being called Mugwe it is the *kiragu* that makes him be called by that name.

11. THE MUKIAMA OF THE TIGANIA. By a Christian elder, GEORGE M. KIRIGIA of Mikinduri.

A section of the Tigania have no Mugwe. Their Mugwe is called Mukiama. He is selected by the elders every three circumcisions (*matana yatato*). Nding'ori, Kubia, and Kaberia selected him because they were about to circumcise their children, and thus he was also to be their envoy (*mutome*) to God (*kere Ngai*).

After his selection, they will always assist him in all his troubles.

In their selection they elect a good elder of the house from which the Mukiama must be selected and they must be sure that he will love his people.

The Mukiama is not like a 'speaker' (*mugambi*) but he is a holy elder selected by God (*mukuru muthure ne Ngai*).

In helping him they do to him the very same things that the others do to the Mugwe.

When it was the time to help them he called their elders (*akiama*) to join in his prayers to God by going to the place of prayer. Not everybody was called, but only the elders (*akiama*), of the prayer, who went there with a ram to offer sacrifice. Where they offered that sacrifice there is a pool (*iria*) and it is in a forest and the name of the forest is *Giitho kia Ukiama*, the wood of the Ukiama. They stayed there expecting that some animal would talk within the pool, and having heard it they

200 THE MUGWE, A FAILING PROPHET

went back to tell their age-class that it had been sanctified (*ibathuriete*) because they had seen something from God. And they remained tied together until they would become *ntindiri*, elders. (See p. 92.)

12. A CURSE BY THE MUGWE. Recorded by my assistant.

A man cannot circumcise his son without first informing those of his lineage and of his class. They must take all kinds of beer, (*maroa, ncobi*), and eat some sheep. Those who will take part in this festival will be of his class and of his set [lit. of the same circumcision].

At the feast, there is no one who cannot go, be they young initiates or women; and they will eat of the sheep.

It happened after one of these feasts, that some were cursed by the Mugwe because they had trespassed his commandments. There is nobody who does not fear these curses of the Mugwe. The Mugwe told them: ' Now, you go because you are evil men.' And those who remained with him were given plenty of food, and they received all the blessings. Those who remained, were those who were free from evil things. There cannot be anyone who is bad with the Mugwe. The others who went away were those who refused to go with the good and that is why the Mugwe cursed them.

And then the Mugwe gave a great feast and he blessed all those who came and they had all kinds of food. After that he told them: ' Now live happily. And the others who went, they will live as they did up to now.'

13. SOME RULES TO BE FOLLOWED BY THE NEWLY INITIATED

1. Do not speak or laugh with other men, but speak with the other initiates.
2. There is nothing whatsoever that an initiate may say he cannot do.
3. Do not turn your back on the road nor overtake women or any other man.

APPENDIX

4. You are not allowed to enter a house, even your own house, unless for food.
5. Cough when somebody comes near to the house.
6. Do not speak with another's mother because she is not his wife. Do not speak with an uninitiated girl even if she belongs to your age set.
7. Do not speak (know) with a girl from your village because she would conceive with shame in the eyes of her people and of others.
8. Do not ask your brother for some meat or ask him to help you in cutting meat.

14. A STORY OF THE 'NUGU' WOOD. A case of Christian reaction to old beliefs. Written by CORNELIO M. MBIJIWE.

This wood of Nugu is found in the Sub-Location of Ng'onyi. There is nothing different inside this wood from the other wood called Mbuguri. Also in this wood there is a great restriction (prohibition) even greater than that of Mbuguri. The Mbuguri wood has its restriction, but this is greater. It is that no man whatever can cut trees in this wood. There is one clan that can cut trees in the wood of Mbuguri, but no clan is allowed to cut even a small branch in this wood.

What is the reason that no one is allowed to cut wood in this forest? Perhaps because there is a water pool inside it. From this pool a small stream runs through the lands of Ng'onyi and Nkomari and joins the Thingithu. Within the year there are months with plenty of rain and months when it does not rain. During these months there is no water in the stream but only at the pool. The months of October–December or *Urugora*, are months when it rains heavily and the rivers are swollen with water, and also this stream is swollen and there is plenty of water. At this time, people will say: 'Look at the Iganka, if it does not run there will be plenty of rain.' This pool is called Iganka, and Iganka is also the name of the water that runs down. Now, how is it that after the rains, water comes down by this stream? When it has rained a great deal, the pool is overflooded and so the water starts running down the stream.

202 THE MUGWE, A FAILING PROPHET

During the months when it does not rain, the ditch is filled with dry leaves and fallen branches. The water is thus obstructed and only when it overflows will carry away all things and the head of the water is covered by all the dry leaves. If it rains heavily during the night, the water in the stream will reach the houses in the early morning, but no one will go out to look at it because no one is allowed to see the head of the water. It is said that that water has its way opened by something like a snake and a lamb of the spirits. For this reason, when the water overflows from this wood, there is much fear and everybody asks when the Iganka will flow.

There are many holes along the ditch, so the water is retarded. If a man happens to see the water there, it is said that the flowing of the Iganka will no longer take place unless a sheep is sacrificed. That man will be earnest in killing the sheep, and so the water, having had time to fill the hole, will overflow and run again; but they will say that the Iganka flows again because of the victim.

There is a place called Kamakie [lit. 'no fear']: if the water is seen after it has flowed over this place, there is no need to kill a goat.

Now, it is from the Nugu wood that the snake and the lamb come out to open the way to the Iganka.

During the year 1950, a teacher was told that the Iganka has stopped not far from his school. He went then with a pupil and they worked with a cutlass (*panga*) in order to free the Iganka. They were advised by the people not to go: ' Do not go, otherwise you will have to offer your sheep.' But they wanted to make sure whether they would fall sick or die, and went where the water flowed over. And they saw the water flow, and they asked themselves: ' Weren't we told that when the Iganka is stopped, even if you open another ditch, the water will not flow? Perhaps we have been cheated. Let us wait now to see the lamb that opens the way to the Iganka.' The water was then flowing through the path. They stayed there in order to see the lamb, and they were prepared to hide themselves if they had seen the lamb. But they did not

APPENDIX 203

see it and were convinced that they had been cheated. Even if the ordinary man refuses to dig a ditch for the Iganka, it remains a falsehood, because they had dug and the Iganka had flowed. In the end they returned to school.

When the elders from Ng'onyi and Nkomari were told of this, they were annoyed and asked whether their boys were going to school for education or for discovering the Iganka. It came about that they no longer allowed their children to go to school for they would go there not for education but for running after the Iganka. The teacher was told that none of their boys was to be touched by the hands that had opened the way to the Iganka, and no house was to be approached by the feet that had trodden on the mud of the Iganka.

The boys left the school until the teacher went to see the headman. And the headman stated that the *njuri* were responsible. The *njuri* were summoned, and they asked for a sheep to be sacrificed before the school could be re-opened. But the teacher knew that the *njuri* wanted a sheep for eating; he said that he was a Christian and that he could not offer a sheep but would report the matter to the Father. The elders realized that the teacher was firm, and they told him to return to his school and teach those pupils he would find there. And that day the school was full to capacity.

But there was resentment among the elders. ' Well, he is a Christian, let us see if that will help him.' They were in fact thinking of A. M. Munyambo, a Christian, who entered that wood to cut some wood, and lost his wits. A. M. Munyambo was an old Christian and he was very good. He fell sick of malaria, but they said that it was due to his entering the wood. When he recovered, his work was to bury the dead. But they said that he was really mad: ' First he entered the wood, now he buries the dead!' So they said that the same fate would now befall the teacher. But since then the teacher has always been in good health and he did not even suffer from the usual sicknesses that trouble the inhabitants of these parts.

This is what the people of the past, and also of the present, tell of that wood, that it contains the things of God.

BIBLIOGRAPHY

Champion, J. W. W., 'The Atharaka', *J.R.A.I.*, XLII, 1912, pp. 68–90.
Based on a month's visit to the Thagichu.

Dundas, C., 'History of Kitui', *J.R.A.I.*, XLIII, 1913, pp. 480–549.
Contains a few notes on the Thagichu.

,, ,, 'The organization and laws of some Bantu tribes in East Africa', *J.R.A.I.*, XLV, 1915, pp. 234–306.
Deals with the Kikuyu, Tharaka (Thagichu), and Kamba.

,, ,, 'Native laws of some Bantu tribes of East Africa', *J.R.A.I.*, LI, 1921, pp. 217–78.
Uses comparative material from the Kamba, Kikuyu, and Tharaka.

Fosbrooke, H. A., 'An administrative survey of the Masai social system', *T.N.R.*, 26, 1948, pp. 1–50.

Holding, E. M., 'Some preliminary notes on Meru age-grades', *Man*, XLII, 31, 1942, pp. 58–65.
Some original information on the organization of women.

Huntingford, G. W. B., *The Galla of Ethiopia* etc. (International African Institute, Ethnographic Survey of Africa), London, 1955.

206 BIBLIOGRAPHY

Lambert, H. E., *The use of Indigenous Authorities in Tribal Administration: Studies of the Meru in Kenya.*
Communication of the School of African Studies, University of Cape Town, N.S., No. 16, 1947.
The Indigenous Authorities are the *njuri.*

,, ,, *The Systems of Land Tenure in the Kikuyu Land Unit.*
Communication of the School of African Studies, University of Cape Town, N.S., No. 22, 1950.
Discusses all the traditions on the migratory movements of the peoples of the Unit, in which the Meru also were then included.

,, ,, *Kikuyu Social and Political Institutions.* Oxford, 1956.
Deals mainly with the age-set system of the Kikuyu, Embu, and Meru.

Laughton, W. H., *The Meru.* Nairobi, 1944.
A good introductory pamphlet in the Series 'Peoples of Kenya', No. 10.

Orde-Browne, G. St. J., *The Vanishing Tribes of Kenya.* London, 1925.

Shackleton, E. R., 'The Njuwe', *Man,* XXX, 143, 1930, pp. 201–202.
Some information on the Tharaka.

INDEX

Abba Boku, 161, *165–168*

Accession, 88, *90–94*, 133

Administration, 4, 27, 28, 170, 173, 174, 176, 184, 187

Adultery, 12, 150

African District Council, 2, 8, 24, 27

Agambi, sing. *mugambi*, 13, 14

Age-set system, 15, *17–24*, 26, 37, 44, 48, 49, 90, 141, 157, 160, 162, 164, 166, 168, 174, 175, 184, 186; age-class, 7, 10, *20–22*, 32, 33, 34, 35, 36, 37, 39, 45, 48, 66, 67, 70, 78, 84, 86, 90, 91, 92, 95, 97, 98, 111, 112, 120, 126, 133, 135, 137, 139, 140, 154, 157, 165, 166, 167, 168, 175, 176, 185, 193, 196, 198, 200; age-set, 21, 171; age-unit, 7, 21

Akiuna, 58, 62, 99

Alternating division, 10, 21, 22, 23, 33, 36, 37, 44, 49

Ancestors, 109, 125, 127, 191

Ariki, sing. *mwariki*, 26

Army, 19, 175

Athwana, *10–11*, 35, 76, 77, 90, 145

Authority, 8, 15, 22, 23, 25, 26, 27, 32, 33, 36, 39, 41, 42, 44, 48, 70, 72, 75, 76, 82, 92, 94, 95, 98, 112, 136, 137, 138, 139, 143, 144, 146, 147, 154, 158, 161, 168, 184, 186, 187, 188, 189

Blessing, 42, 45, 105, *110–118*, 120, 127, 129, 133, 134, 136, 137, 138, 144, 154, 155, 157, 160, 165, 175, 183, 188, 193, 195, 196, 197, 200

Blood-brotherhood, 5, 12, 16, 17, 56, 57

Boran, *see* Galla.

Bridewealth, 13

Candidate, 41, 44, 45, *82–86*, 87, 105, 106, 133, 138

Champion, A. M., 18, 22

Changing order, 169, 186

Chief, 2, 28, 40, 45, 59, 61, 62, 75, 82, 95, 130, 137, 138, 139, 142, 143, 144, 154, 155, 163, 166, 170, 175, 180, 184, 187, 191, 197, 198.

Christian,—Meru, 20, 27, 29,—Oath 27, 185, 203. *See also Missions*.

Chuka, 2, 3, 4, *5–6*, 11, 16, 20, 23, 24, 25, 28, *43–46*, 49, 77, 78, 81, 83, 84, 86, 88, 89, 90, 93, 96, 97, 99, 105, 109, 110, 119, 132, 133, 143, 145, 147, 152, 157, 175, *177–181*, 183, 192, 193, 199

Circumcision, 5, 6, 17, 21, 111, 167, 183, 193, 195, 196, 199, 200

Clan, 6, 7, 9, 11, 12, 14, 15, 16, 42, 47, 48, 58, 59, 62, 70, 78, 82, 83, 99, 113, 120, 140, 143, *147–150*, 151, 163, 192, 193, 196, 198, 201

Clitoridectomy, 17

Comba, 39, 70, 170, 171, 175

Commandments, 140, 200

Continence, 107

Councils, 2, 7, 13, 14, 15, 20, 23, 24, 27, 37, 47, 89, 94, 123, 139, 147, 150, 151, 152, 153, 154, 155, 156, 157, 167, 184

Creation, 51, 52, 54

Crown, 95

Cultural heroes, 52, *62–67*, 72, 75, 82

Cursing, 12, 121, 122, 137, 148, 149, 196, 200

Custodian, 160

Death, 13, 15, 26, *88–90*, 125, 139

Democracy, 23

District, 1, 2, 3, 4, 5, 6, 7, 9, 28, 29, 176; -Commissioner, 1, 2, 172, 173; -Officer, 7, 28; Division, 9; Location, 1, 4, 5, 6, 9; Sub-Location, 1

Diviner, 33, 34, 35, 46, 47, 63, 77, *131–136*, 146

Drunkenness, 107, 108

208 INDEX

Dual divisions, *9–11*, 145
Dundas, C., 11, 18, 41

Elderhood, 108, 150, 175, 178, 179, 180
Elders, 8, 12, 13, 15, 19, 20, 22, 23, 25, 31, 35, 36, 37, 38, 41, 42, 45, 47, 50, 56, 63, 69, 70, 72, 75, 76, 78, 79, 80, 82, 86, 87, 88, 91, 94, 95, 96, 98, 99, 100, 101, 103, 105, 107, 108, 112, 115, 118, 120, 126, 127, 133, 135, 136, 138, 139, 141, 143, 146, 147, 148, 149, *150–155*, 161, 165, 169, 170, 171, 173, 174, 175, 176, 178, 180, 183, 186, 188, 195, 196, 198, 200, 203
Embu, 1, 2, 6, 47, 48, 195, 196
Emergency, 6, 7, 8, 24, 28, 44, 178, 181, 193
Eriatune, 58
Esoteric, 96, 99, 101, 104, 175
Europeans, 39, 55, 56, 122, 141, 170, 172, 176, 196
Exodus, 3, 9, *56–62*
Exogamy, 10, 12, 16

Family, 12, 14, 15, 18, 44, 70, 71, 77, 82, 85, 86, 95, 100, 108, 119, 120, 142, *147–150*, 159, 161, 167, 197; -Unity of the Agwe, *77–82*
Father, 136, 139, 147, 151, 158, 160, 164, 166, 188
Fees, 100, 111, 128, 143, 150, 183; for initiation to *njuri*, 25, 186
First-born son, 41, 82, 83, 84, 85, 105

Gaaru, *18–20*, 22, 86, 97, 111, 112, 140, 154, 155, 156, 172, 175, 183, 195
Gacurwa, 46
Gada system, 166, 167, 168
Gaita, 58, 62, 99
Galla, 4, 161, 162, 165, 166
Gerontocracy, 23
Giciaro, 16, 193. *See also* Blood-brotherhood.
Gicuthi, 69, 70, 72
Githarike, 171, 172, 173
God, 16, 33, 34, 38, 52, 53, 55, 61, 62, 73, 91, 92, 94, 101, 107, 109, 113, 115, 116, 117, *123–128*, 129, 131, 132, 136, 138, 139, 159, 160, 164, 188, 194, 195, 199, 200, 203
Guarantor, 160, 164, 188
Gumba, 6, 192

Hayu, 161, *165–168*
Hereditary principle, Succession, 34, 38, 41, 44, 77, *82–85*, 105, 132, 133, 138, 143, 158, 163, 167

Holiness, 139
Honey, 7, 43, 66, 67, 143, 198
Honey-beer, 43, 92, 95, 98, *100–101*, 110, 128, 193
Hood, 95, 98

Iboka, 63, 64, 65, 80
Identification, 144, 159
Igande, 17
Igembe, 3, 4, 5, 10, 16, 18, 20, 22, 24, 25, 27, 28, *31–35*, 37, 47, 49, 57, 68, 78, 80, 81, 84, 87, 90, 92, 96, 97, 98, 99, 100, 106, 110, 119, 132, 133, 135, 146, 147, 151, 152, 157, 160, 165, 167, 168, 178, 180, *184–186*, 193, 199
Igoji, 3, 4, 5, 46, 146
Igoki, 9, 10, 11, 35, 36, 54, 90, 114, 145
Iguru, 68
Ikwenga M. Ithaing'u, 36
Imenti, 3, 4, 9, 16, 17, 20, 22, 24, 27, 28, 31, *38–40*, 43, 49, 57, 66, 67, 74, 78, 80, 86, 87, 88, 89, 90, 93, 96, 97, 101, 102, 103, 104, 107, 110, 111, 112, 114, 115, 117, 118, 120, 121, 122, 126, 131, 132, 133, 143, 146, 150, 157, 169, 171, 172, 173, 174, 176, *181–182*, 198
Initiates, 18, 19, 20, 54, 106, 111, 129, 140, 154, 155, 156, 157, 171, 174, 185, 187, 193, 195, 196, 197, 200
Initiation, 12, 14, 15, 17, 18, 25, 26, 27, 106, 111, 137, 139, 158, 164, 176, 183, 184, 185
Insignia, 92, 93, *94–104*, 135, 143, 150, 160, 197
Itinerary, 114–115
Itumbiri Mucung'a, 37

INDEX

209

Jaluo, 192
Judge, 122-123

Kabaka, 192
Kaberia, 22
Kamba, 2, 6, 41, 47, 68, 69, 100, 131
Kamundi, 43, 73, 112, 113, 119, 120, 123, 124, 127, 129, 175
Kangangi, 171, 172
Kiama kia Kiiru (Mbiru), 26; kia Nkomango, 20; kia Nkome, 26; kia Ramara, 20; kia Ruamba, 26
Kiboka Falls, 63, 65
Kiganka, M. Kanata, *43-46*, 78, 81, 82, 83, 84, 86, 96, 98, 99, 109, 119, 143, 152, 175, *177-181*, 183, 184
Kikuyu, 1, 2, 6, 8, 41, 57, 89, 104, 113, 123, 131, 172, 193
King, 76, 86, 109, 127, 143, 157, 161
Kipsigis, 173
Kiragu, 38, 39, 43, 54, 56, 61, 62, 74, 95, 101, 110, 111, 128, 143, 150, 169, 170, 173, 182, 197, 199
Kirirwa, 38, 102, 143, 150, 181, 182
Kiruka, 21
Kirurwa, 68, 69, 70
Komenjue, 57, 60, 62, 75
Konguru, 40

Laibon, 161, *162-165*, 173
Lambert, H. E., 2, 3, 16, 17, 20, 23, 24, 48, 56
Land-Unit, 1, 177
Laughton, W. H., 20
Left hand, 61, 74, 103, 110, 120
Lenana, 163
Lineage, 12, *14-15*, 19, 82, 83, 85, 86, 102, 103, 113, 129, 133, 139, *147-150*, 151, 156, 158, 159, 197, 198, 200
Litany, 34
Lumbwa, 192
Lunyiru, M. Ithiria, *33-35*, *132-135*

Magical character, 164, 165
Mantle, 92, 95, 96, 97, 98, 103, 108, 110, 135, 193
Marriage, 12, 13, 14, 20, 106, 107, 125, 139

Masai, 5, 123, 161, *162-165*, 173
Mau Mau, 6, 7, 28, 44, 119, 155, 179, 181, 193
Mbatian, 163
Mbere, 2, 5, *47-48*, 68, 69, 193
Mbwa, 2, 5, 6, 9, 47, 52, 54, 56, 57, 59, 76, 81, 105, 140, 191, 192
Medicine-man, 41, 42, 47, *128-131*, 162, 163, 164, 187. *See* Mugaa.
Meru, 1, 2, 3, 7, 14, 15, 16, 17, 18, 20, 22, 24, 28, 29, 40, 47, 48, 50, 52, 55, 56, 57, 60, 62, 63, 66, 67, 69, 71, *75-76*, 85, 89, 95, 102, 104, 109, 111, 120, 123, 125, 128, 131, 136, 141, 155, 157, 158, 159, 160, 161, 162, 166, 167, 170, 171, 172, 176, 177, 182, 184, 187; educated 26, 27, 28, 94; Town, 4, 28
Military activity, 156
Missions, 4, 7, 28, 29, 37, 39, 182
Miutini, 3, 4, 5, 46
Moral character, 77, 137, 138, 158, 188
Mugaa, 128-131, 156, 157, 186, 187. *See also* Medicine-man.
Mugambi Baituuru, 32, 84, 99, 102, 144, 152, 186
Mugwe, *passim*—; assistant, 36, 43, 145
Mukagunda, 62
Mukanyaki, 62
Mukiama, 11, 35, 37, 38, 77, 91, 114, 126, 144, 146, 185, 199
Mukithiriini, 62
Mukuna-Ruku, *73-74*
Mukunga, 79
Murungu, 34, 113, 114, 123, 124, 126, 127, 132
Mutethia, 62
Muthambi, 3, 4, 5, 16, 20, 23, 46, 47
Muthetu, 58, 62
Mutuampea, 40, 70, 71, 89, 111, 120, 122, 153
Mwimbi, 3, 4, 5, 23, 24, 28, 46, 47, 48, 74, 141
Mworia, 46
Mythology, 50, 67, 73, 74, 75, 76, 77, 79, 82, 105, 148, 158, 159, 170

INDEX

Nandi, 173
Ndinguri, 22
Ngai, 34, 123, 124, 126, 134
Ngitira, M. Athongu, 38, 181
Ngua ntune, 58
Nguve, 6.
Njuri, 2, 7, 8, 13, *24–28*, 44, 119, 150, 151, 152, 157, 184, 185, 203
Nkeya, 111, 153
Nkomango, 20, 27
Nkuene, 9
Nkuru, 172
Ntangi, 66
Ntiba, 21
Ntindiri, 13, 39, 60, 91, 94, 138, 139, 159
Ntuiko, 21, 22, 23, 24, 32, 33, 35, 38, 45, 90, 92, 96, 97, 111, 112, 145, 154, 155, 157, 186

Orkoyot, 173
Ownership, 11, 12

Pankratio Mureethi, 44
Parental authority, 15, 16, 137, 139, 161
Personal tax, 143
Piron elders, 165
Political authority, 8, 9, 13, 15, 137, 139, 140, 158, 165, 166, 167, 168, 186
Polygyny, 10, 15
Poor, 110, 116, 117, 129, 130, 176
Power, 2, 8, 13, 61, 62, 75, 76, 82, 90, 92, 99, 102, 105, 110, 113, 130, 133, 136, 137, 138, 145, 146, 148, 149, 150, 157, 158, 160, 165, 168, 174, 184, 185, 196, 197, 198; of the Mugwe, 61, 62, 70, 72, 73, 77, 94, 103, 121; of the Ugwe, 67, 105, 135, 140, 141, 142, 144
Prayers, 112, 114, 115, 116, 123, 127, 129, 130, 133, 134, 164, 199
Priest, 127, *136–140*, 161
Primogeniture, 82–85, 147
Prophet, 31, *136–140*, 161
Prophets, 53, 54, 55
Puberty, 17
Purity, 105, 106, 107
Raids, 10, 19, 119, 128, 154, 155, 157, 162, 175, 195

Rain, 13, 102, 114, 115, 116, 148, 162, 164, 197, 201, 202
Rainfall, 7; rain-maker, 116, 148
Ramare, 20
Religious character, 137, 138, 158, 165
Rendille, 16, 56, 57
Rima, 66
Rite, 110, 112, 113, 139
Ruanda M. Mwoga, 40, 41, 70, 71, 79, 81, 98, 101, 108, 111, 119, 127, 153, 154, 183, 184

Sacred honey, 43; —things, 43
Sacrifice, 13, 107, 108, 109, 110, 113, 114, 115, 117, 123, 125, 133, 138, 139, 164, 167, 199
Sanctions, *118–122*, 123, 125, 137, 154, 168, 188
Schools, 19, 28, 29, 176, 183, 185, 202, 203
Secrecy, 19, 26, 65, 68, 104, 173
Secret societies, 26, 174
Sendeyo, 163
Shackleton, E. R., 6
Shrine, 100, 101
Sponsors, 19
Staff, 36, 58, 59, 61, 95, 99, 100, 135, 140, 144, 178, 191, 194, 196
Stone, 119, 120
Stool, 94, 95
Sub-clan, 12
Sub-tribes, 3, 4, 7, 8, 9, 13, 16, 20, 22, 23, 28, 30, 46, 49, 57, 63, 67, 71, 76, 77, 78, 81, 82, 90, 92, 95, 101, 104, 105, 112, 123, 125, 128, 133, *141–147*, 149, 151, 154, 157, 158, 159, 160, 161, 163, 164, 165, 172, 177, 182, 184

Tail, 63, 64, 69, 72, 73, 194, 195
Thagana, 11
Thagichu, 1, 42, 72, 99, 144
Tharaka, 1, 3, 5, 6, 7, 11, 12, 17, 18, 20, 22, 24, 26, 28, *40–43*, 47, 49, 55, 57, 59, 63, 64, 67, 69, 70, 71, 72, 76, 78, 79, 80, 85, 88, 89, 90, 93, 98, 100, 108, 109, 110, 112, 113, 116, 119, 121, 122, 123, 126, 127, 128, 131, 133, 139, 140, 144,

INDEX

147, 148, 149, 153, 157, 172, 173, 174, *182–184*, 193, 195, 198, 199

Thathi, 21
Thieves, 120, 121
Tigania, 3, 4, 5, 10, 11, 16, 20, 22, 24, 28, *35–38*, 49, 58, 59, 65, 76, 77, 78, 80, 88, 90, 92, 96, 97, 98, 99, 100, 114, 126, 132, 133, 144, 148, 157, 160, 165, 167, *184–186*, 193, 199
Tribal unity, 1, 7, 8, 57, 76
Tribe, 1, 3, 6, 7, 8, 13, 57, 128, 141, 162, 164
Tumbiri, 11
Turkana, 56, 57, 192

Ugwe, 8, 32, 39, 41, 43, 44, 47, 48, 68, 69, 70, *75–76*, 77, 78, 79, 80, 81, 82, 86, 99, 101, 106, 126, 130, 135, 141, 142, 143, 147, 151, 158, 161, 175, 177, 178, 181, 182, 184, 193, 199
Umetho, 10, 11, 35, 42, 49, 119, 144
Urio, 2, 10, 11, 35, 42, 49, 57, 76, 80, 98, 119, 144, 183

Virtues, 78, 83, *105–109*

War, 16, 162, 167
Warriors, 20, 46, 98, 99, 109, 111, 112, 113, 119, 128, 129, *155–157*, 162, 167, 170, 175, 183, 185, 194
Witchcraft, 174
Women, 110, 118, 112, 133, 134, 135, 139, 191, 196, 200
Wrath, 120

Youth, 17, 18, 175